EARLY INDONESIAN TEXTILES

EARLY INDONESIAN TEXTILES FROM THREE ISLAND CULTURES

SUMBA·TORAJA·LAMPUNG

Robert J. Holmgren

Anita E. Spertus

THE METROPOLITAN MUSEUM OF ART
DISTRIBUTED BY HARRY N. ABRAMS, INC.
NEW YORK

Published in conjunction with the exhibition
Early Indonesian Textiles from Three Island Cultures:
Sumba, Toraja, Lampung, held at The Metropolitan
Museum of Art, New York, February 14–May 14, 1989,
and at The Textile Museum, Washington, D.C.,
June 17–August 6, 1989.

Published by The Metropolitan Museum of Art, New York
John P. O'Neill, Editor in Chief
Barbara Burn, Executive Editor
Emily March Walter, Editor
Michael Shroyer, Designer
Matthew Pimm, Production

Color photographs taken by John Bigelow Taylor.
Maps drawn by Wilhelmina Reyinga-Amrhein.
Sketches drawn by Anita E. Spertus.

All works in the exhibition are in the collection of
Robert J. Holmgren and Anita E. Spertus.

Composition by U.S. Lithograph, typographers, New York
Printed and bound by Colorcraft Lithographers, Inc., New York

On the cover: One face of a two-sided pennant (No. 1).
  Sumba, ca. 1900

Library of Congress Cataloging-in-Publication Data

Holmgren, Robert J.
  Indonesian textiles from three island cultures: Sumba,
  Toraja, Lampung/Robert J. Holmgren and Anita E. Spertus.
      p.   cm.
  Exhibition catalog.
  Bibliography: p.
  ISBN 0-87099-538-3.—ISBN 0-8109-2424-2 (Abrams)
    1. Textile fabrics, Sumbanese (Indonesian people)—
Exhibitions. 2. Textile fabrics, Toraja—Exhibitions.
3. Textile fabrics, Lampung (Indonesian people)—Exhibitions.
I. Spertus, Anita E. II. Metropolitan Museum of Art (New
York, N.Y.) III. Title.
NK8980.A3S8755   1989
746'.09598'07401471—dc19   88-38613
                                            CIP

The black-and-white photographs, where they are not credited
in the captions, are reproduced through the courtesy of the
following institutions: Figs. 1, 11, Martinus Nijhoff, Dordrecht;
Fig. 2, Museum voor Volkenkunde, Rotterdam; Figs. 6, 7, 14,
A. A. Balkema, Rotterdam.

CONTENTS

FOREWORD

Rarely does a society invest textiles with intense religious significance, and yet accord them primary importance as indicators of temporal wealth and status. Such, however, has been their role for centuries in Indonesia, where weaving, the work of women, was a counterpart to sculpture and jewelry, created by men. Like painting in other cultures, textiles assumed an esteemed place as the greatest of two-dimensional art forms in Indonesia, where painting was almost nonexistent. Far beyond their customary utilitarian roles—as clothing, for example, or furnishings—textiles have been employed by the peoples of Indonesia in potent emblematic and sacred contexts.

These textiles from tribal Indonesia cast an immediate spell; the vibrancy and beauty of their color and the unfamiliarity of their imagery evoke a visceral response mixed with wonderment. Far from appealing simply as decoration, they project in some instances the same dynamism as modern abstract art, in others a subtly sophisticated classicism. The many-layered significance of their designs gradually reveals itself, both visually and in the complexity of their powerful symbolism. Ancient Indonesia was the hub of trading systems, and a pathway for religious and artistic influences, which conveyed exotic patterns and forms throughout Indonesia's thousands of island populations, supplementing and modifying patterns already millennia old. Images deeply embedded in the ancient neolithic traditions of Indonesian peoples combined with designs acquired from other Asian civilizations to create a rich iconographic tradition which celebrated a cosmology founded on a pantheon of gods, a population of revered ancestors, and a universe teeming with supernatural presences. Textiles were central to the tasks of mediating between mankind and this often dangerous or terrifying universe, and of maintaining a balance that kept them in their due positions.

With the rapid erosion of Indonesia's traditional cultures, its fragile legacy of textiles is not being renewed. We are fortunate to have the opportunity to exhibit a selection of works from Sumba, Toraja, and Lampung from the collection of Anita E. Spertus and Robert J. Holmgren, which has a legendary reputation among students of the subject. It is the harvest of many years of patient work and exacting discrimination. They have previously lent individual masterpieces to exhibitions, but have never before shown as many at one time. The selection contains many hitherto unknown textile genres, new even to specialists. We are grateful to them for this view of a magnificent but little-known field, and for the scholarship that informs their text.

The inspiration for this exhibition we owe largely to the constant enthusiasm of Cynthia Hazen Polsky, Trustee. Members of the Museum staff who have contributed curatorial care are Douglas Newton, Evelyn A. J. Hall and John A. Friede Chairman of Primitive Art; Nobuko Kajitani, Conservator in Charge, and Christine Giuntini, Assistant Conservator, of the Textile Conservation department; and Jeffrey L. Daly, Chief Designer, who was responsible for the installation.

Philippe de Montebello
Director

PREFACE

We first encountered Indonesia in books, during a period when we were wholly absorbed by the art and history of India's Brahmanic, Buddhist, and Islamic cultures. In 1973, we undertook the excursion—obligatory sooner or later for Indianists—to mainland and island Southeast Asia, an area that scholars used to call, with undisguised condescension, "Further India," because Indian influence is visible or predominant in many artifacts of ancient periods, and because some of its societies were affected by Indian religion, language, customs, and ideas of statecraft during a long era (A.D. 100–1800) of cultural interaction. Our immediate destination was central Java's eighth-century Borobudur temple. At that time—just before the most recent restoration of this monument and its disquieting transformation into a tourist park—we found ourselves intimately alone on an immense man-made mountain, day after day, wrapped in early morning fog or revived by light afternoon rains, climbing stone terraces that progressively depict, in exquisitely carved reliefs, the stages of spiritual growth. Moved by the piety and ravishing beauty of this Buddhist monument, we realized with growing astonishment that ancient Javanese artists had, at least as monument builders, "outmastered" their Indian masters. But did Borobudur and other Indian artifacts and lingering "Further Indian" traits necessarily imply that Indonesians had become (another old term) "Indianized"? Even a temple as Indian in style as Borobudur was subtly different: on the sculpted terraces of this stupa—and, we noticed, in the twentieth-century Javanese environment around it—we saw a pervasive kindness, a modesty and gentility, a sweet human smile that we had not observed in Indian art except from a much earlier time—at Sanchi perhaps, another Buddhist "mountain where divinity dwells," or in other great works of India's Sunga and Kushan periods.

Intending to stay one week in Indonesia, we remained for three months, unable to wrench ourselves away. Wandering about, without real goal, first in Java and then from island to island in this living museum of mankind, we acquired the rudiments of the language, kept to villages rather than the modern cities, walked rather than rode as much as possible. We marveled at the lush garden land, at the grace and dignity of its people, and were astonished by the panoply of cultures, each with its own depths. We found a diversity of artistic expression and interpretation, far less "Indian" than we had anticipated—indeed, not Indian at all—but simply tinged by much that was familiar from other great Asian civilizations. Our initial impression—of peoples that had adopted foreign styles without necessarily adopting their foreign significations, and had changed them, "Indonesianized" them, and applied local meaning to them—intensified during this and many subsequent visits. That first encounter abruptly changed the direction of our lives; Indonesia became an obsession, and its relationship to the larger Asian world of which it is and has been an active part dominated our thoughts thenceforth.

Gradually, our focus narrowed to the central issue of iconographic roots: Where did Indonesian patterns and forms come from? If they are not innate to the people and country, then when did they arrive? Who brought them? Why do the same designs appear in so many widely scattered cultures? Why were they appealing to Indonesians? Do the meanings they hold for modern villagers relate to their original significations? What were those meanings?

From the outset, it was apparent that textiles were the best available tool for exploration of these questions. Every Indonesian people, it seemed, had been making them for a long time. Women—far more traditional, village-bound, and conserving than men—designed, wove, and owned them. Even if the textiles themselves were not ancient, they were astonishingly retentive of iconography that was, in some cases, two thousand years old. Most important, in many local contexts where all trace of older forms of sculpture and architecture either lay in desuetude or had disappeared, textiles were still tucked in chests and cupboards. They were, in fact, relatively plentiful, and, furthermore, large study collections of old material were available in Dutch institutions. And precisely because Indonesia was entering an historic phase of dramatic change, of modernization and development, the moment had arrived when villagers were drawn to the future and relinquishing the past, in a radical break with tradition. Not infrequently, the pieces that were most important for our purposes were those which villagers, and the marketplace in general, valued least: old "broken" cloths, fragments that represented, in our eyes, pieces which fit an emerging puzzle, or clues in the reconstruction of what very early Indonesian textiles must have looked like. For art-historical purposes, it is virtually axiomatic that, in an environment such as Indonesia, where only stones and metal last for more than a century or two, truly old objects inevitably sustain some damage (and conversely, objects in perfect condition are seldom old).

Some of the results of our inquiry are offered in this volume. For many reasons, we have generally tried to maintain some distance from the anthropological approach that begins (and usually ends) with local usages and local interpretations of iconographic meaning. Very often, regional meanings for textile patterns are simply unavailable—nobody remembers, or the answers of villagers are obviously speculative (this is particularly true of older textile types which have lapsed into disuse). The underlying problem is that few textile patterns were recently invented or adopted; most are very old, and copied—latterly, rather blindly—through the ages. Although customary and ritual usages of textiles bearing particular patterns sometimes persist, we often find unrelated usages for the same patterns in different cultures, perhaps because the Balkanization of the archipelago caused the common practices and ideas of former times gradually to diverge.

We prefer to search for visual correlations between cultures, for potential donor-recipient relationships, and then to seek historical periods in which common experiences or motivations might have touched the cultures involved. Anthropologists today tend to study narrow localities, an intensive approach that yields far more detailed and useful information than older cross-cultural methods; but in the Indonesian arena, they have produced little in the category of art history.

An important caveat concerning this volume is that it weds a generalizing art-historical text to a narrowly focused art collection—an uneasy union, because private collectors are seldom guided by the comprehensive criteria that institutions commonly embrace, but rather by the freewheeling indulgence of personal aesthetics, of preferences, prejudices, and skews of focus that can plunge them into particular areas of interest at the arbitrary expense of others. If we ascribe foreign influence to a disproportionate number of objects herein, it reflects our collecting priorities and subjective interests, which in turn suggested the theme of this book. In our view, these influences greatly enrich Indonesian art, without diminution of its "Indonesianness."

Brief catalogues for the general reader and exhibition-goer regrettably do not offer scope for the extended argumentation and comparative illustration that we would have liked to include, to support our conclusions. Moreover, our initial intention to pursue a thread of discussion that would develop in complexity and depth was somewhat thwarted by the requirement that each catalogue entry stand on its own. For these very serious shortcomings, we apologize.

Many people have contributed—some unwittingly, others with unwonted energy—to the making of this book. Most important are the teachers, so numerous that to endeavor to name them risks many omissions. A few, however, were crucial. Georg Tillmann gave us, through his superb collection of Lampung material (now in the Tropenmuseum, Amsterdam), an indispensable source of ideas and sheer visual delight. In 1964, the brothers Laurens and Jaap Langewis issued, with a few perfunctory words, a subtle pictorial teaching—the best and deepest kind: a book about aesthetics (*Decorative Art in Indonesian Textiles*) that grows and ripens subliminally, and to which we have returned time and again to seek and find additional insight. Their discriminating eyes have immeasurably enriched the collections of museums across Europe and Japan; when these storehouses are inspected, Langewis textiles always stand apart, reflecting a recognizable and sympathetic taste. To the distinguished Javanist K. R. T. Hardjonagoro we owe another lasting debt for a different type of subtle teaching, the deep traditional Javanese kind, in words we scarcely comprehended when he spoke them, but which gathered nuance and asserted their truth in subsequent years, as we delved deeper into very different areas. His ecstatic understanding of both textile history in a Javanese perspective and Indonesia's ability to absorb, manage, and profit from foreign ideas while preserving always the original Indonesian essence, colors many of the arguments presented in these pages. The late comparative ethnographer Carl Schuster has been our most provocative mentor; Schuster epitomized an approach to art history generally considered antiquated even in his own time; but in our view, his time is still to come.

Cynthia Hazen Polsky, Trustee, conceived and inspired the Metropolitan Museum's recognition of Indonesia as an important world culture; without her insight and inexhaustible energy, this exhibition would not have come to pass. Douglas Newton, Chairman, Primitive Art, brought the exhibition to fruition; together we spent many absorbing days examining hundreds of textiles, in order to arrive with mutual satisfaction at the present small selection. His discernment, diplomacy, and constant friendship were a joy. The Metropolitan is staffed by uncommonly gracious professionals, many of whom contributed unstintingly to this project. Nobuko Kajitani, Conservator in Charge of the Metropolitan's Textile Conservation department, has been for many years a connoisseur of Indonesian textiles; with painstaking help from Christine Giuntini, Assistant Conservator, she prepared the objects and designed all mounts for the exhibition, which was installed to best visual advantage by Jeffrey L. Daly, Chief Designer. Barbara Burn, Executive Editor, Editorial Department, supervised a tight and abbreviated schedule with humor, toleration, and sensitivity. Authors are often loath to divulge the whole truth about the role of their editor, because were they to do so, the editor's name would appear perforce, not in fine print—sandwiched somewhere between the copyright and the C.I.P. data—but next to the writers' own. In this instance, Emily March Walter worked with us day and night for more than three months to refine this text; her dedication and professionalism under great pressure exemplifies the aspiration of the Museum itself, for the very best possible. Michael Shroyer designed these pages with a keen eye and sympathy for the material. Matthew Pimm coordinated technical details of production; his perfectionism is especially evident in the faithful color reproductions. Wilhelmina Reyinga-Amrhein skillfully drew the unconventional maps. Jean Wagner edited the bibliographical citations with painstaking care. John Bigelow Taylor took the beautiful color photographs.

Lastly, our sincere thanks to professional friends, for collegiality, discussion, advice and instruction, and other contributions which they will each, individually, recognize: Soedarmadji J. H. Damais, Mattiebelle Gittinger, Perry Kesner, Brigitte Khan Majlis, Pierre-Yves Manguin, Robyn Maxwell, Carolyn Owerka, Imelda Ridwanto, T. T. Saklofsky, Garrett and Bronwen Solyom, Jef and Christine Vanderstraeten, A. M. L. R. Veldhuisen-Djajasoebrata, Kent Watters, and finally Doris Wiener, a fine teacher who for a decade gave us the extraordinary opportunity to see, handle, and study in depth, day by day, many profoundly moving masterpieces of Indian religious art.

INTRODUCTION

Ancestral spirits pervade Indonesian life. They inhabit special precincts of the everyday world, of worlds beyond, and of the mind. Spirits appear in dreams and trances, or as apparitions; they make themselves known in the direction of a bird's flight or in the carefully analyzed entrails of a pig. Times of day, cardinal directions, transitional periods in individual and social life, crucial labors such as weaving or harvesting, rituals that ensure fertility, health, power—all are highly charged and subject to the intercession and active participation, for good or ill, of spirits. Consequently, peoples throughout the Indonesian archipelago are concerned continually with their medial position between an upperworld of deified ancestors and gods, and a watery netherworld of crocodiles and lizards, of earth and fertility. The human drama —life and death, fulfillment and sorrow, prosperity and misfortune—reflects the balanced polarities of, and interacts with, these spirit worlds. Mankind strives to remain in continuing contact with the supernatural realms, to harmonize with them, and to incline the spirits to aid and advise.

Textiles, almost all of which are made by women, play a critical role in maintaining harmony and balance between spirits and humanity. They are not capriciously patterned or merely decorative. In their display and accumulation, they connote measurable degrees of wealth, status, and power; but in their inspiration, realization, and use they are inseparably bound to deep religious convictions.[1] The objects in this volume are all hieratic; they display spirits, totems, geometric emblems charged with significance, or scenes from myth. The presence of these images in textiles serves specific functions: protection, guidance, supplication, remembrance.

Most often, weavers meticulously copied old prototypes known to be efficacious by virtue of the powerful patterns encoded in their yarns. Every stage of the process—collection of dyestuffs from shrubs and plants, harvesting of cotton, fixing of patterns, dyeing, weaving, finishing—was regulated by strict procedures, and observed by tutelary deities who guarded the cotton field, made the dye react, guided the maker's fingers, or gave mental clarity and repose. Through offerings to the spirits, meditation, sexual abstinence, purifications, observance of taboos, and other austerities, the weaver sought to maintain an elevated, concentrated, and tranquil state of mind while work progressed. Sometimes, the inspiration for design inventions arrived in dreams or visions. The weaver might feel spiritually and physically endangered until the spirits materialized in her cloth, newly balanced in power and form. In Borneo, for example, a freshly inspired design entitled its creator to be honored with the same thumb tattoos as a headhunter: her communion with spirits and ancestors and his blood offering together assured the common weal.[2]

Devout temper shaped the process of creating cloth, just as conviction determined the pattern and divine service the use. For important textiles women rarely employed facile techniques, such as printing or painting, but clung instead to difficult, time-consuming procedures, because they were sanctioned by tradition and deepened the inner quality of the pieces, and because the making of the cloth was itself a religious expression. Resist- (or reserve-) dyeing techniques, used so extensively in Indonesia that their local names (ikat, batik, pelangi) have been adopted worldwide as generic terms, require that the real work of patterning (binding with fiber, or the application of paste or wax, in order to "resist" the penetration of the dye) be undertaken in negative design areas. The immersion of yarns or finished cloth in dye baths yields the color of positive areas. These technical imperatives engender, in both weaver and viewer, a persistent awareness of the interdependence between foreground and background. Other complicated techniques require that weaving halt after each pass of the shuttle, so that selected warps may be handwrapped one at a time (No. 45), or that threads be laid in so that no warp or weft pattern-float is visible on the reverse (thus, single-faced textiles such as Nos. 15 and 16). Some genres seem excessively complex in their construction, which possibly indicates the presence of an archaic technique, or an effort to emulate the weave of foreign fabrics. Nos. 21 and 22, for example, carry dozens of discrete supplementary weft yarns for four or five meters from one warp end to the other, creating thousands of selvedged centimeter "slits" that are then tied and dyed after weaving.

For Indonesians, textiles serve not merely as apparel or fashion; they connote the essential civility and humanness of a person, which distinguishes him from beasts. In Java, an infant who survives his first precarious weeks of existence is clad in a single thread, to certify his incorporation within the human community. At every stage of life henceforth, particular patterns and colors will signify rank, clan affiliation, age, marital status, wealth, and spiritual orientation. Special weavings protect or empower the wearer at moments of communal danger or individual instability. A few cloths, the most spectacular, appear only on major ceremonial occasions that renew clan identity and unity. In death, shrouds may depict the food, riches, livestock, servants, and other requisites that a bereaved clan provides for the soul's passage to, and life in, the next world, as well as emblems of identity that will enable recognition (No. 17). Other shrouds declare the dead man's membership within a network of ancestral kin (No. 25).

Many important textiles are never worn, but are suspended as banners (Nos. 1, 23) or displayed like paintings (Nos. 36–39), ennobling and sanctifying the spaces in which they hang. Others serve as dowry treasure, tribute, temple offerings, or tokens of solicitation. Some are supernaturally empowered to protect, heal, render invincible, or alter destiny and shape events. Borneo headhunters slept under charged cloths in order to accumulate power before a raid; they sang lullabies to trophy heads swaddled in specially woven *sungkit* shawls, or determined events from an animal's innards while their head and shoulders were shielded by a *sungkit* canopy (No. 45). Sometimes the same cloth would perform at many different moments of passage, from receiving a baby out of the womb, to pillowing a corpse. The splendid pictorial environment of *tampan* (Nos. 29–34) envisions an entire community as a ship at sea, a corporate body that organizes and subordinates individual roles to the triumphal progress of the whole.

Viewed together, the textiles illustrated here are strikingly dissimilar from one another in appearance. Indeed, "Indonesian textiles" is an essentially misleading label which covers a large group of cloths that are often only distantly related, while other equally pertinent pieces (from the Philippines, Taiwan, Malaya, the Pacific, continental Southeast Asia, and Madagascar) are arbitrarily excluded from the category. "Indonesia" as a linguistic, cultural, and ethnic entity extends far beyond the boundaries, determined by European colonial politics, of the modern Republic. The original Indonesian "home-land" is usually located by historians in the far northeast (in prehistoric south China, and then, at the very beginning of history, in Taiwan or the Philippines). Thus, Indonesian peoples first spread south, and thence both east and west, across vast island-dotted ocean areas, from Hawaii to the east African coast (see map, page 16). Today, the westernmost areas of the Malay Archipelago constitute the heartland of these peoples: Sumatra, Malaya, Java, and the coasts of Borneo and Celebes. The accelerated development of societies on these large islands and peninsulas was due to their control of richer lands and resources, and to greater contact with other peoples and material cultures. In general, textiles and other decorative arts increase in sophistication as one proceeds westward from the small eastern islands—where traditional textiles consist mainly of rough cotton decorated with plain weave stripes or simple decorative motifs—to an island such as Sumatra, with its wealth of techniques, materials, and visual effects. Weaving is a distinguishing trait of this greater "Indonesian people"; among groups ethnically or linguistically unrelated to Indonesians (that is, the aboriginal inhabitants who survive in isolated areas), weaving traditions are generally undeveloped or absent, as in New Guinea.

The variety of visual expression in Indonesia is the result of disparate historical experiences. The archipelago is a strategic crossroads between great civilizations to the northeast and the northwest. A vast array of foreign peoples, ideas, and products has funneled through Indonesia's straits and called in her ports for thousands of years, sowing changes in the culture both gradual and cataclysmic. Peoples originally united in outlook gradually diverged in their religious beliefs (with the arrival of Hinduism, Buddhism, and Islam), absorbed populations from other regions, were devastated by enemies, or were eclipsed by volatile market tastes. These experiences affected the islands unevenly and at different times; but one common consequence was the physical and psychological "withdrawal" of particular cultures from the creative coastal forefront to the less accessible—usually volcanically mountained, densely jungled—interior, which effectively slowed or suspended their cultural evolution. Some societies that had been active participants in the flow of pan-Indonesian

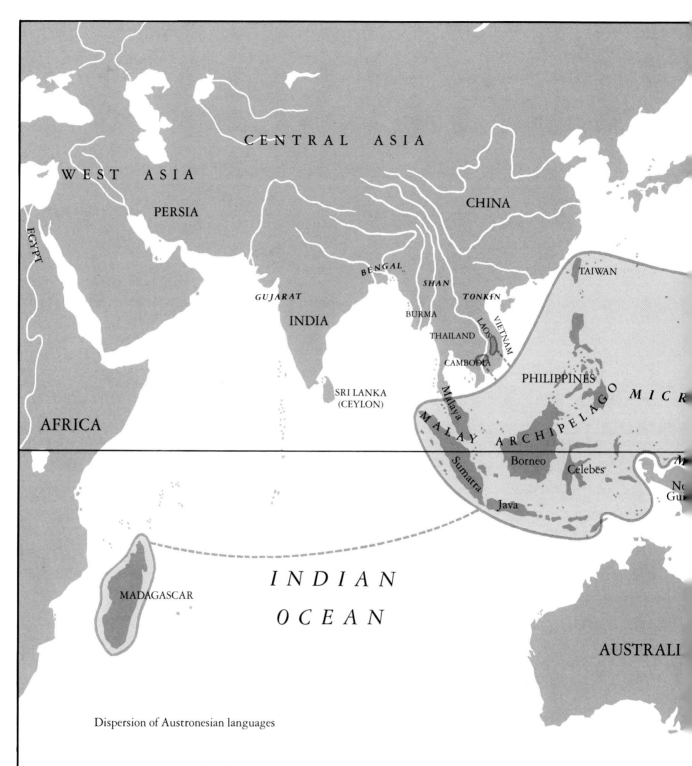

CENTRAL ASIA

WEST ASIA

PERSIA

EGYPT

GUJARAT

BENGAL

SHAN

TONKIN

BURMA

VIETNAM

LAOS

INDIA

THAILAND

CAMBODIA

CHINA

TAIWAN

SRI LANKA
(CEYLON)

PHILIPPINES

MICR

AFRICA

Malaya

MALAY

ARCHIPELAGO

Sumatra

Borneo

Celebes

N

Ne
Gu

Java

INDIAN

OCEAN

MADAGASCAR

AUSTRALI

Dispersion of Austronesian languages

Maritime World of Asia and the Pacific Showing the Present Distribution of Austronesian Peoples and Languages

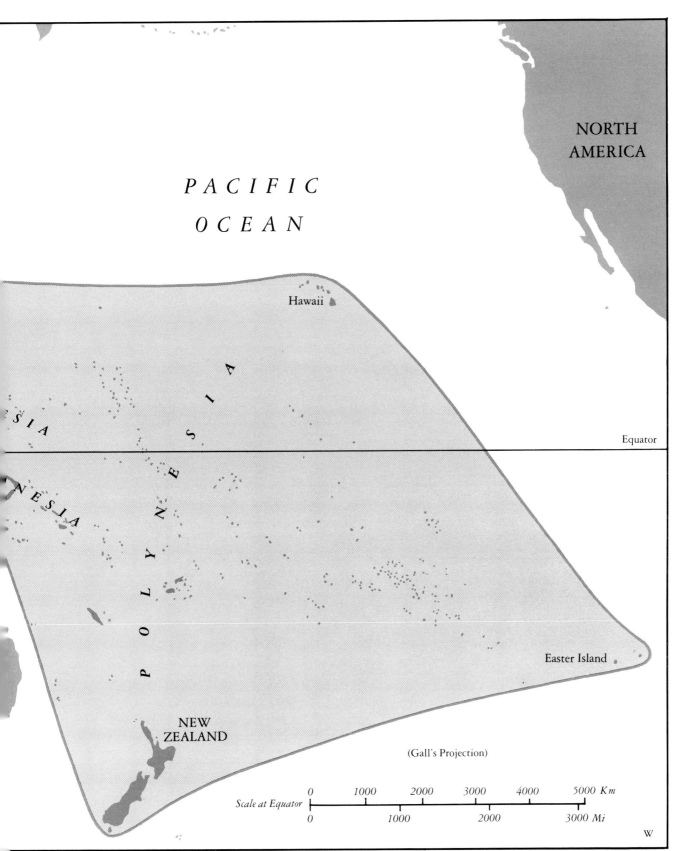

PACIFIC

OCEAN

NORTH
AMERICA

Hawaii

ESIA

SIA

NESIA

P O L Y N E S I A

Equator

Easter Island

NEW
ZEALAND

(Gall's Projection)

	0	1000	2000	3000	4000	5000 Km
Scale at Equator						
	0	1000		2000		3000 Mi

W

Sources: [Jakarta] 1938; Bellwood 1979; Bellwood 1985.

history fell aside as cultural backwaters, frozen in the Bronze Age. Others enjoyed continuous exposure to external traditions, and developed a veneer of sophistication. In a sense, Indonesia is like a living museum, embracing societies that occupy every stratum in the development of human culture. Textiles reflect these varied historical experiences, like visual fossils.

Indonesians frequently adapted and reinterpreted for their own purposes imported designs, often finding iconographic meaning and figural form in what appear to be abstractions (No. 15). The relationship of these reinterpreted images to their original sources is further obscured by centuries of elaboration. However, by comparing the various designs from different islands, those common root elements may be discerned despite dramatic differences of scale, color, and character. The occurrence of nearly identical iconography on the textiles of Indonesian and Southeast Asian peoples who live thousands of miles apart, and who could not plausibly have had any direct contact with each other, helps to distinguish source patterns from adaptations (Nos. 29–35). These parallels prompt a search for vehicles that could have carried iconography to places distant from one another, for the mediums in which they originally appeared, and for the reasons they were embraced by so many cultures. Religion, namely Buddhism, seems in many cases to have been both the vehicle and the compelling reason.

This volume focuses on three cultures with visually dramatic textile traditions: east Sumba, a small island in south-central Indonesia; Toraja, the sprawling interior region of Indonesia's fourth largest island, Celebes (Sulawesi); and Lampung, the southernmost area of Sumatra, confronting the coast of west Java. Comparing them, one sees first, not the subtle stylistic variations of a culturally united people, but radically different approaches to design, shaped by a profound historical fragmentation of the archipelago's inhabitants. This impression is, however, ultimately superficial, for deeply embedded beneath the differences, a vision held in common can be discerned, which reflects shared cultural beginnings.

Small islands situated near trade routes were extremely vulnerable to commercial and political manipulation; but a few outlying islands such as Sumba, with small, relatively homogeneous populations and scant economic attraction, retained their cultural integrity while still enjoying broadening and fertilizing interrelations with many other Indonesian and foreign peoples.

Sumba textiles are syncretic and heavily indebted to imported imagery, but also full of references to local life. Although Sumba received and interpreted with refinement diverse trade patterns, many of its most memorable images are neither genteel nor delicate, but proud, proclamatory, raw, often sexually candid, or violent. Human or quasi-anthropomorphic images (Nos. 1–3) peer out of Sumba's past—stark ancestral presences; skull trees and naked men mingle with a *patola* motif borrowed from an elegant Indian silk (No. 17); glorious gold ornaments sculpt miniature warriors armed to kill (No. 6). Yet there is (or once was, before Sumba was transformed by commercialism) much more to Sumba textiles than picturesque drama. Sumba too remembered very old forms (the Cycladic purity of Nos. 12, 13); it valued imagery imbued with courtly refinement (Nos. 9–11); it was a brilliant interpreter of geometrical pattern (No. 15); it preserved trade patterns that were introduced in a Hindu-Buddhist context more than a thousand years ago (Nos. 7, 8).

Interior regions, such as Toraja, isolated from the outside world and often surrounded by adversaries, have retained early design traditions that are close to ancient sources. To find in other cultures corollary patterns that might have influenced or inspired Toraja design, we must cast back to China during the Han dynasty (206 B.C.–A.D. 220) and even earlier—an astonishing continuity considering the relative age of extant Indonesian textiles, which is seldom more than one hundred fifty years.

The main Toraja weaving regions of Galumpang and Rongkong were totally destroyed and their populations exiled during civil insurrections from 1951 to 1964. Cultural artifacts and their communal context both were lost. Christianity and Islam forcibly replaced the animist beliefs that informed the iconography and usage of ritual weavings, and the essential reason for making such cloths therefore disappeared. Nineteenth-century observers failed to explore the significance of textile patterns in Toraja culture, and because almost no early examples remain, information about the meaning of designs is now virtually unavailable. In recent years, however, early weavings have emerged from several other Toraja regions that were largely spared the disruptions of the 1950s, and to which the Galumpang and Rongkong people traditionally traded their textiles until the early twentieth century. These textiles include familiar Galumpang and Rongkong genres, but also unknown types that suggest the existence of heretofore unrecognized weaving centers in north Toraja, among the Palu and Poso Toraja (No. 28).[3]

Toraja textiles radiate power. An impression of sheer size is conveyed even when the actual scale is small (though Torajans also made the largest cloths in Indonesia—No. 24 exemplifies the type). Torajans *saw* monumentally; it comes as no surprise that Toraja is one of the few scattered sites in Southeast Asia where enormous megalithic sculptures were erected. Toraja textile patterns are always exuberant, uncompromising, direct—never extraneously ornamental, and rarely figural. Execution is painstaking and precise, as in the razor-sharp ikat and burnished finish of No. 25, or the technical complexity of Nos. 21 and 22. Each Indonesian weaving culture has its own distinctive range of reds; Toraja shades have a warm orange glow, like embers in a forge (No. 25), or a lovely cherry tone (No. 28). Rhythmic, metrically paced, Toraja textiles seem consciously framed to draw the eye in progressive stages directly to the center, where balance and repetition develop an extraordinary tension.

Coastal Indonesians, such as those living in Lampung, assimilated textile traditions from many places, both from within and from without Indonesia. Lampung is situated immediately adjacent to, and has often been part of, the most important kingdoms in Indonesian history: Tarumanegara (fifth century A.D.), Srivijaya (seventh century), Pajajaran and Majapahit (thirteenth century), and Banten (sixteenth century). Lampung oversees the Strait of Sunda, one of

MALAYA

SOUTH

CHINA SEA

Malacca Strait

BATAK

SUMATRA

MINANGKABAU

Palembang ○

PASEMAH

KOMERING

LAMPUNG

Kenali ●

Palas
Pasemah

Semangka
Bay

Kalianda ○ ▲

Lampung
Bay

KRAKATAU

Sunda Strait

Banten ○

IBAN

J A V A

JAVA

TARUMANEGARA
PAJAJARAN

Cirebon ○

M A J A P A H I T

S U N D A

Borobudur ▲

J
A
V
A

Majapahit ▲

Gre ○

Wonosari ●

○ Cities

● Villages

▲ Historical sites and *STATES*

□ *ETHNIC GROUPS*

▬ *ETHNIC BOUNDARIES*

I N D I A N

O C E A N

Western Part of the Malay Archipelago

CELEBES

SEA

SANGIR

BORNEO

• Bentenan

CELEBES

Makassar Strait

PALU □

POSO □

GAJU

T O R A J A

GALUMPANG □

MAMASA □ *RONGKONG* ■

□ *SA'DAN*

BURU

BUGIS

S E A

B A N D A

SEA

BALI

WETAR

Sembiran
•

Selaparang

B A L I ▲

SASAK

SUMBAWA

FLORES

LOMBOK

TIMOR

SUMBA

*EAST
SUMBA*

| 100 | 200 | 300 | 400 | 500 *Km* |

| 100 | 200 | 300 *Mi* |

W

Sources: [Jakarta] 1938; Kruyt 1938; Van Royen 1930.

the two waterways through which international maritime trade flowed between East and West; its counterpart, the Strait of Malacca, debouches near Lampung's east coast. Cavalcades of ships sailed past Lampung over many centuries, and were recorded, with verisimilitude, in her textiles. With a few minor exceptions, Lampung weaving ceased at the end of the nineteenth century.

Indonesia's most painterly weavings are found here—delicate masterworks of fluid line, naturalistic description, and saturated color, married to a complex figural iconography. Our knowledge of the meaning of these literal, detailed images remains scant. Hence, Lampung textiles have a mysterious character, not because the weavers did not necessarily understand the iconography they were copying, but because of our own lack of comprehension of the implied narrative, and because the forms themselves suggest such a wide range of evocative associations.

Few Indonesian cloths predate the nineteenth century. Tropical weather, rodents and insects, and the tradition of taking important cloths to the grave have destroyed earlier examples. In Indonesia, replenishable old goods tend to be used up, not sanctified. When Galumpang Toraja were exiled in the early 1950s, they carried with them not their own beautiful weavings (burnt along with their houses, fields, shrines, and sculptures), but mediocre old Indian trade textiles, which they believed to be gifts from the gods. Other primary sources of information about early textile traditions are also lacking. Dutch colonial records chronicle increasing Western involvement in politics, pacification, and trade from 1600 onward, but scarcely mention local Indonesian culture until the nineteenth century. European missionaries, often the first outside observers, though occasionally earnest reporters of a passing way of life, were inherently charged to destroy those very beliefs and customs. Few Indonesians were collectors of their own cultural artifacts in the Western sense of connoisseurship, although many accumulated imported goods (e.g., porcelain). But Indonesia's very magnitude (thirteen thousand islands dotting eight thousand kilometers of atoll and reef-ridden water) strained the limited administrative resources of Holland, with the result that many of these cultures remained relatively undisturbed until quite recent times. Their destruction (or "development") proceeds today at a rapid pace.

Although many Indonesian textile patterns arrived from abroad, the favored designs, those to which the islanders constantly return, are very old and, if not indigenous, long naturalized. It seems likely that many powerful totemic images (No. 1) and mythical scenes (Nos. 18, 20) belonged originally to the pre- or proto-historic Austronesians, who brought them from earlier homelands to the north (No. 19), whereas elaborate geometric or pictorial patterns (Nos. 9–11, elements of Nos. 17, 29–34, and 45) were originally non-Austronesian. Foreign imagery came on bronzes, illuminated manuscripts, coins, trade textiles (possibly including carpets), pottery, paintings, and other artifacts. Although trade played the central role in this dissemination of images, its economic importance was essentially marginal because it was devoted exclusively to luxury items beyond the reach of all but aristocrats. Other objects arrived with pilgrims and embassies, as dowry and ceremonial gifts, and as plunder (piracy was as widespread as, and almost indistinguishable from, commerce).

Indonesians absorbed these styles and images over millennia; they digested them, transformed details, palette, scale, format, medium, and meaning, and recast them in threads and cloth. Women wove with summary power: their warps and wefts bound together the beliefs, the magic, the legendary episodes and glorious aspirations, the dreams and fears, and the healthy and malignant powers of their societies. Cloths often can be read like historical texts, which, in conventional form, are for the most part absent in Indonesia. At the same time, textiles intimately express the inner sensibilities of these women, their poetry, their perfectionism and patience, and their love for this odd but great art with the unique power to communicate by enveloping and embracing us.

1. In this volume, we frequently use the "ethnographic present," which describes often idealized conditions, practices, and beliefs that once "originally" obtained, as if they still operated with full effect. In truth, times have changed. Indonesia is eagerly modernizing. The weaving communities have all been affected. Some early customs and beliefs still prevail, in whole or in part, depending upon the island or region; but they are fast disappearing, and, in fact, no great textiles are produced anywhere in Indonesia today.
2. Vogelsanger 1980, p. 121.
3. See also Khan Majlis 1984, eighteenth and twenty-second color plates following page 160.

SUMBA

1. ONE FACE OF A TWO-SIDED PENNANT (*PENJI?*)
   WITH LIZARDS

East(?) Sumba
ca. 1900
Imported cotton fabric, trade beads, string
58 × 34 cm (23 × 13½ in.) [↕] *

This pennant, depicting an anthropomorphized lizard symbolic of sexuality and concupiscence, celebrates life and fecundity. Wrists, elbows, and knees—which Sumbanese believe are repositories of energy—bulge. Splayed fingers and toes quiver with life. Mouth and genitals, unstitched to the cloth backing, are left to flap freely. Flanking the lizard are crabs and lobsters which, with their capacity to regenerate limbs, are symbols of rebirth. Two white fetal forms crouch, their arms and legs tucked close. The brash frontal form of the lizard, its peaked head, orant pose, and spread fingers resemble Stone Age cave paintings of coastal New Guinea (fig. 1).

Several east Sumbanese clans believe that crocodilian creatures are among their original ancestors, or *marapu*, through marriage and sexual intercourse. Accordingly, crocodiles are revered; they may not be killed or eaten; nor do they harm people, unless an individual has committed an offense against a clan descended from crocodilian *marapu*. Young aristocrats are called "children of the crocodile and whale," or "sea turtle, red crocodile." Crocodilian creatures "are thought to inhabit a large village beneath the sea, where they assume human form. Formerly, it is said, crocodiles were friendly and co-operative towards humans, transporting them across rivers on their backs. . . . The treachery of a man called Kapilandu, 'deceiver,' led to the breach of this amicable relation."[1]

The red cotton fabric of this pennant is imported. Throughout Indonesia, red is generally associated with earth, women, fertility, and blood. In Sumba, the menses are called *wai kombu*, "red liquid," after the root of the *kombu* tree, source of the dye used in traditional Sumbanese textiles. Sumbanese believe that conception occurs in the mingling of white male semen and red female blood. They relate red to marriage, danger, phenomena deemed "hot," the sun, sacrifice, and death—a list associated with the various significations of blood.

Beaded bands with similar dimensions (No. 14) are usually affixed to plainwoven *lau* sarongs, but it was reported that this pennant and its nearly identical companion were originally stitched back-to-back and hung in front of a house on ceremonial occasions.[2] This conjecture is supported by the vertical orientation and the finishing features at warp ends, though other examples of the genre are unknown.

1. Forth 1981, pp. 224, 100–101, 444 note 42.
2. Donald Friend, Sydney, personal communication, 1976.

Fig. 1. Cave painting. Duri Cave, New Guinea. After Van Heekeren, *The Stone Age of Indonesia* (1972), plate 72

* Dimensions are given in centimeters and inches, warp preceding weft.

   [↔] and [↕] indicate the orientation of the warp in photographs.

2, 3. TWO *LAU HADA* (WOMEN'S CEREMONIAL
       SKIRTS WITH SHELLS)

Cotton, trade beads, nassa shells; appliqué,
plied fringe

2. Reportedly from Bolobokat, central Sumba
   Early 20th century
   Male and female images on opposite sides
   (female illustrated)
   56×79 cm (22×31 in.) [↔]
   Exhibited: "Splendid Symbols: Textiles and
   Tradition in Indonesia," Textile Museum,
   Washington, D.C., 1979.
   Published: Gittinger 1979, no.124a,b; Holmgren
   1979, p. 25; Gittinger 1980, p. 119.

3. East or central Sumba
   Late 19th century
   Twill
   Female images on both sides
   The bead panels were cut in Sumba from their
   original sarong and applied to an early twentieth-
   century sarong.
   60×83 cm (23½×32½ in.) [↔]

The gigantic male and female figures that preside on
opposite sides of *lau hada* No. 2, probably an ancestral
couple, are sculptural and hieratic.[1] As in the cave
painting noted in No. 1 (fig. 1, page 26), a peering X-ray
vision discloses their internal bone structure. Reptiles,
chthonian creatures associated with fertility, lick the
figures' genitalia and, mounted astride ponies with
exaggerated sexual parts, squeeze their waists. Large
crocodilian creatures flank the shell-and-bead figures,
like mysterious counterparts or consorts. Described in
shaggy plied fringe brown as the earth, they tremble and
sway, shadowy presences that emerge from the netherworld to brush the radiant couple with earth's life-giving
waters.

    The more naturalistic style of the figure in *lau hada*
No. 3 suggests that it predates No. 2. Its image of
woman is modest rather than coolly heroic, somewhat
gangly of limb, and unprepossessing. The belly is softly
rounded, and the face, crowned by the traditional spiky
coiffure, is depicted more realistically. Ribs and genitals
burst out of the body (compare fig. 2), and nipples,
navel, and clitoris are golden. *Mamuli*, traditional omega-
shaped ornaments (see also Nos. 4–6), here convey
explicit female symbolism: they appear as earrings and
(unique in our experience) define the shape of sexual parts.

Sumba's nineteenth-century traffic in horses generated large new revenues for her princes,[2] stimulating the production of increasingly ostentatious textiles lavished with costly imported materials (nassa shells and beads—which circulated as money—coins, madder-dyed Indian materials, and chemical-dyed threads imported from Europe) that flaunted wealth and implied power (impoverished aristocrats were not respected[3]).

1. Both sides of *lau hada* No. 2 are reproduced in Gittinger 1979, no. 124a,b (in color in 1985 ed.).
2. Adams 1969, pp. 5–6, 8. The Dutch prized Sumba's ponies as cavalry stock, and established their first permanent station on the island in 1866 to ensure a steady supply of mounts.
3. Forth 1981, p. 464 note 24.

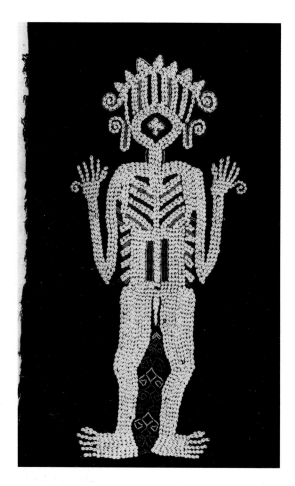

Fig. 2. *Lau hada* depicting male figures; obtained on Sumba by D. K. Wielenga 1913–21. After Adams and Djajasoebrata, *Leven en dood op Sumba* (1965), p. 15 (reverse illustrated in Adams 1969, fig. 21)

4–6. THREE *MAMULI* (EAR ORNAMENTS
OR PENDANTS)

East Sumba
19th century
Gold

4. Trees festooned with buffalo horns
   Height 9.6 cm (3¾ in.)
   Exhibited: "Indonesische Textilien," Rautenstrauch-Joest-Museum für Völkerkunde, Cologne,
   1984–85.

5. Two cockatoos
   Baing village, south coast of Sumba
   Height 7.7 cm (3 in.)

6. Two warriors
   Kanatangu district
   Height 9.8 cm (3¾ in.)
   Exhibited: "Indonesische Textilien," Rauten-
   strauch-Joest-Museum für Völkerkunde, Cologne,
   1984–85.

Oral tradition associates the distinctive omega-shaped form of *mamuli* with female genitalia. In earlier times, when lobes were stretched by heavy ear ornaments, *mamuli* hooked through the distended holes.[1] Both sexual symbolism and usage are visually explicit in *lau hada* No. 3. Today, *mamuli* are worn as pendants.

Mamuli play an essential role in the elaborate gift exchanges that weld Sumba society together. In marriage negotiations, for instance, the groom's gift of metal goods (deemed masculine) to the family of the bride must be reciprocated by a counter gift of textiles (feminine).

To the Sumbanese, precious metals are of heavenly origin: the sun is made of gold, the moon and stars of silver, "deposited in the earth when the sun and moon set and when a star falls from the sky."[2] Gold possessions (ornaments and coins) signify wealth and divine favor. Elaborate *mamuli*, which number among the sacred relics housed in the recesses of the clan treasury, serve to maintain contact with ancestors and spirits.[3] "These are almost never taken out of the dark, for fear that their huge powers would kill onlookers and bring natural disasters. . . . It appears that these jewels are the very essence of the lineage and its political and religious powers."[4] As grave goods, *mamuli* accompany the soul to the land of the dead.

It is not known whether fancy gold *mamuli* were actually made on Sumba. Although Sumba men smith,[5] the technical and stylistic uniformity of many older *mamuli* suggests routine workshop production, while the very finest examples were probably the work of specialized artisans. Such *mamuli* may have been imported from nearby islands, or made by resident Chinese.

No. 4 displays lofty "skull trees" (see also No. 17). The branches are studded with the heads of slain enemies; the trunk is embellished with buffalo horns. East Sumbanese envision clan lineages as trees, of which ancestors and, by inference, the centrally located ancestral house (in which the deceased clan founder still resides among his sacred relics) constitute the trunk. Forked stakes, places of animal sacrifice and vestiges of megalithic culture found throughout much of Southeast Asia, rise beside the *mamuli* trees.[6]

No. 5 is the oldest and most beautiful of these three *mamuli*. Its gold has a reddish glow. Surfaces are volumetric; delicate spiral ornament enlivens each edge. The two cockatoos, mouths agape, are wild-eyed, their head feathers flying upward. Lovely necklets adorn their throats, and a flower cup and cluster of berries rise to their beaks.

No. 6 depicts warriors clad in wrapped turbans and loincloths, striding forth as to battle. Arms flex; heads swivel in their sockets; brandished swords and shields pivot at the shoulder. Smaller figures accompany them in supplicating attitudes.

Mamuli-shaped ornaments, usually gold or silver, are found throughout central and east Indonesia. Archaeological examples, sometimes bronze or iron, have been found in graves on, among other islands, Java and Sumatra (see text, No. 44).

1. See Adams 1971, p. 35, and Rodgers 1985, p. 173 for photographs of Sumbanese wearing *mamuli*-shaped earrings.
2. Forth 1981, p. 441 note 7.
3. Rodgers 1985, pp. 172–77.
4. Ibid., p. 174.
5. Forth 1981, p. 16.
6. See Van Suchtelen 1919, fig. 65 (cf. Rodgers 1985, fig. 19).

7, 8. TWO *LAU PAHUDU* (WOMEN'S CEREMONIAL
SKIRTS)

Rotated ninety degrees from their orientation
in use.

7. Parai Yawangu village, Rindi, east Sumba
ca. 1905
Cotton; supplementary warp, daubing, plied
fringe, appliqué
60 × 74 cm (23½ × 29 in.) [↕]
Exhibited: "Textile Traditions of Indonesia,"
Los Angeles County Museum of Art, 1977

8. Pau village, Umalulu (Melolo), east Sumba
ca. 1875
Cotton, trade beads; supplementary warp,
daubing, plied fringe, appliqué
56 × 79 cm (22 × 31 in.) [↕]

Sumbanese manipulate supplementary warp with masterly finesse. Zigs and zags tremble, as if the figures they describe breathe. Grooves of pattern trace musculature and sinews, or articulate knuckles and haunches. A yellow dye, daubed after the textile is woven, recalls the gilding of ancient cloths described in Sumba oral literature[1] (many prized textiles from west Indonesia are gilt). This golden yellow tone accents parts deemed "hot": sensory organs, knees, ankles, armpits, and genitalia.

In *lau pahudu* No. 7, an aristocratic lady is borne upon an elephant and sheltered by a parasol. At far left, a "tree" rises from a column of hexagonal medallions; at right lofty foliage appears, or possibly the elephant's lustration. Elephants and umbrellas are esteemed symbols and accoutrements of paramount power throughout the Indianized world.

Lau No. 8 predates No. 7: the rich Turkey-red dye of the appliqué trade cloth is plant-derived rather than chemical; beads resonate together with the ground in an old subtle color harmony; and brown daubs occur in two delicate tones rather than one. But above all, it is the complexity of the scene, the press of detail, the integration of human characters within the whole, and the honeyed glow that support an early date.

Two male figures command the prows of a ship; a great fruiting tree of life rises between them, and a horse is shown in the hold. The original trade-textile source pattern on which No. 8 is based probably depicted prows with bird or serpent heads, an image widely reproduced in west Indonesia but apparently never assimilated in Sumba. The bird prows are now highly stylized; birds perched in the central tree are also reduced to abstraction.

Some Sumba villages have a tripartite ship-shaped plan of "prow," "midship," and "rudder."[2] Ship imagery also occurs in Sumba myth and ritual. Prior to planting, there is a series of prayer feasts led by a royal priest that culminates in the narration of a ship's voyage from the upperworld to Sumba by the divine founder of the noble lineage—the birth of the clan.

One of the preliminary rites requires that a large sacred textile be spread out on the roof "to dry in the sun"; subsequently, functionaries climb to the peak [of the village temple] carrying the textile and two small ancestor post-figures (male and female) which are to be installed on the ridge of the roof. Below, the priest calls out the names of the places which are the same as those given . . . in the account of the voyage. . . . After each group of names the priest calls out to the man at the top, "Do you see them?" Holding the textile in his lap, the man who is seated behind the male ancestor looks out into the beyond and cries, "Yes, I see them." The exchange continues until the present village name is reached, following which the various clan Elders take fire from the temple to relight their own hearths and the temple is officially opened.[3]

Before the harvest, another myth is recounted, concerning "a [king-]hero who ascends in a boat or on a horse through the eight levels of a magic plant in order to reach the Upperworld where he wins his heavenly [queen-]bride. The magic plant possesses leaves of flowered textiles (*rau patola*) and fruit." When a king dies, he is wrapped in layers of textiles and borne in a boat-shaped wooden container that will take him to "the Otherworld where the sun goes down."

Sumba designs usually organize unrelated motifs in geometric harmony.[4] Here, by contrast, the images are interrelated, verging on complete narrative scenes and suggesting a world of rich early traditions now lost.

The quaint proportions of the elephant in No. 7 suggest that the weaver had never seen this creature, and indicate that the Sumbanese did not invent this tableau imagery but adapted it from trade textiles.[5] On Sumba, the imagery was reinterpreted with naked vitality and empowered with local associations: regenerative crabs (here, seen beside the parasol) and prestigious ponies. The central anthropomorphic figure—brazen, larger than life, and native to Sumba—almost certainly supplants an original passenger of more genteel, diminutive aspect.

7

Fig. 3. Sumba *pahudu* (pattern guide), used to preserve supplementary warp design. Bamboo and cotton. Collection Anita E. Spertus and Robert J. Holmgren

No other Sumba textile known to us displays iconography similar to that of No. 8. *Lau pahudu* are precise copies of patterns preserved on *pahudu* (heirloom pattern guides, fig. 3). By nature, *pahudu*-based iconography changes only gradually, if at all. This specific boat tableau probably evolved from images on textiles that circulated centuries ago throughout mainland Southeast Asia, and west and central Indonesia; those ancient prototypes are now lost, but iconographic imprints of them survive on local reproductions made by widely scattered cultures.[6] Almost certainly, the original prototypes were either commercial trade items or religious articles of foreign manufacture. Despite shared elements, today's Southeast Asian derivatives are very different from one another in overall appearance, which implies a long period of local evolution. The probable period for the original dispersion of iconography like that seen in Nos. 7 and 8 is beginning first millennium to beginning second millennium A.D. These are very early dates, almost unthinkable a decade ago and still essentially theoretical, but supported by a growing body of research.[7] (See also Nos. 29–33.)

1.   Adams 1969, p. 88.
2.   Ibid., pp. 342–43.
3.   Adams 1974, pp. 335–36.
4.   See, for example, No. 17; Langewis and Wagner 1964, plates 118–46.
5.   For comparable Indian *patola* (silk double-ikat) elephant images, see Bühler and Fischer 1979, motif types 13–15, 19–22; Holmgren and Spertus 1989b. Elephants in similar contexts also appear in supplementary weft technique on textiles from other Southeast Asian cultures.
6.   Some lineal descendants of prototype trade textiles are Sumatran *tampan* (Nos. 29–34), Lombok ritual cloths (No. 35), skirt cloths from Sumbawa (Langewis and Wagner 1964, plate 116), Cambodian ikat breast cloths, and Thai and Laotian weft-patterned shawls (Cheesman 1988: compare the top center illustration on page 106 to No. 7, and the bottom illustrations to No. 8).
7.   See Gittinger 1989; Holmgren and Spertus 1989a.

8

9–11. THREE TUBULAR DECORATED BANDS FROM
LAU PAHUDU

East Sumba
Second half of the 19th century
Cotton; supplementary warp, daubing, plied fringe

9. Displayed area 53 × 27 cm (21 × 10½ in.) [↔]

10. Displayed area 57 × 24 cm (22½ × 9½ in.) [↔]

11. Displayed area 53 × 27 cm (21 × 10½ in.) [↔]
Exhibited: "Indonesische Textilien," Rauten-strauch-Joest-Museum für Völkerkunde, Cologne, 1984–85.

Supplementary warp bands for *lau* were often made separately, then stitched to plainwoven skirts. Few of these lyrical bands survive. Plied supplementary yarns grip the tightly woven infrastructure and provide durability, but the sarongs to which the bands were once attached—often dyed black with earths that oxidized—have disintegrated in almost every case. The delicate handling and elaborate rhythmic brocadelike patterning of these *lau* bands suggest a date contemporaneous with or slightly earlier than *lau* No. 8. Band No. 9 is purely abstract and remains close to its *patola* source (the same pattern that inspired *paporitonoling* No. 27). Nos. 10 and 11 cast an intriguing light on the process by which spirits materialize from abstract elements to the animist eye: faces seem to peer in rows along No. 10, and lizards crouch among the tendrils of No. 11.

These and similar bands underscore sharp distinctions between nineteenth- and twentieth-century Sumba weaving. Elaborate figural textiles were formerly far less common; geometric patterns, which sometimes embodied subtly concealed human and animal forms (see, for example, No. 15), were more the norm. The commercialization of Sumba weaving, with a market-oriented premium on fantastic figural patterns, had not yet begun when these bands were made; but by the early twentieth century, most Sumba women were weaving for trade.

Ornate and sophisticated, Sumba textiles stand dramatically apart from other east Indonesian traditions, which are often limited to plainwoven stripes, wiggly lines, and an occasional *patola* pattern for variation. Sumba cloths clearly belong to a different design mentality, the so-called *pasisir* tradition of west Indonesia (see text, Nos. 29–33). Early trade textiles bearing designs like those on *lau pahudu* Nos. 7 and 8 or the present *lau* bands presumably reached Sumba also from the west. Some Sumba clans assert that their ancestors came originally from Java, which claimed nominal sovereignty and probably commanded considerable prestige in east Indonesia before the sixteenth century. Sumba legends describe the expulsion or enslavement of an indigenous population by newcomers who became the ruling class.[1] An elaborate set of weaving taboos reserved the preparation and use of highly decorated textiles to the aristocracy—strictures that disintegrated only as commerce in textiles accelerated in the late nineteenth century. East Sumba cloths, and *lau pahudu* in particular, may be an unrecognized source of information about the visual appearance of textiles during the precolonial period, precisely because they follow old pattern guides and therefore discouraged iconographic innovation.

1. Forth 1981, pp. 238; 466 notes 3, 5; 217.

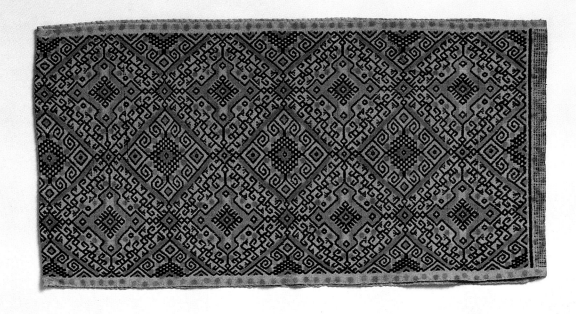

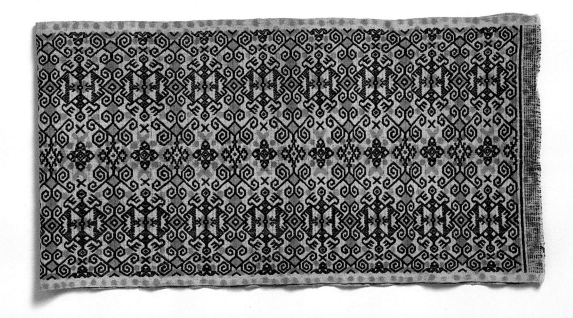

12, 13. TWO *KATANGA NJARA* (FITTINGS FOR
     A HORSE BRIDLE)

    East Sumba
    19th century or earlier
    Cast bronze

    12. Height 11.7 cm (4½ in.)

    13. Height 9.8 cm (3⅞ in.)

Consistency of visual form pervades traditional societies.
These Brancusi-like anthropomorphic objects reportedly
joined the headstall straps of a bridle. They were probably conceived as male and female. Archaic, and monumental in expression despite their small size, they
incorporate the same angular, figural shape as *mamuli*
(Nos. 4–6), with clear reference to sexual parts (see
also No. 3).

14. Appliqué band from a *Lau Katipa*
(Woman's ceremonial skirt with beads)
with dancing horses

East Sumba
Late 19th century
Wool, cotton, trade beads
67 × 45 cm (26½ × 17½ in.) [↔]

Sumba has long been renowned for her ponies which, together with sandalwood and textiles, provided a strong and continuous trade link with other peoples. Horses are the most costly and desirable component of east Sumba gift exchange. In certain rituals, horses were said to dance trancelike on their back hooves.[1] The direct inspiration for these crowned, rearing steeds may have been images engraved on European, Dutch East India Company, or Netherlands East Indies coins, which were widely circulated throughout the colonial period. However, rampant confronting zoomorphic motifs have been seen throughout Asia since classical antiquity, perhaps seeding a favorable predisposition to the heraldic images on Dutch regalia.

1. In Java, "dancing" horses are well documented (Pigeaud 1938, pp. 215–43).

15, 16. TWO BELTS

East Sumba
19th century
Cotton; supplementary weft float (visible on one face only)

15. Belt, 64 × 12 cm (25 × 4½ in.) [↔]

16. Belt, 71 × 10 cm (28 × 4 in.) [↔]; accompanying pouch, 13 × 9 cm (5 × 3½ in.) [↔]

These archaic textiles exemplify the process of reinterpretation, whereby elements from a complex foreign source, when experienced in a different cultural context, are infused with fresh life in local production.

Dense passages of belt No. 15 appear at first to be abstract geometric brocade patterns. Closer inspection, however, reveals that slight, purposeful adjustments to these symmetrical designs have engendered spirits and figures (see detail, page 44). At left, slender horses parade, with spiky manes, gaping mouths, sway backs, and turned tails (fig. 4a). Lanky stick figures descend one from the other (fig. 4b; see also discussion of genealogical flow in Nos. 25 and 41). Pairs of orant men with shared heads squat sideways within the pattern (fig. 4c), and large crocodiles float at right, defined by circular heads and elongated tails (fig. 4d). Other creatures are art-historically imminent: squids, birds, and human figures—fully realized at a later date—here appear in prototype, on the cusp of transition from abstract source material to figuration.

The process of reinterpretation and clarification is illustrated in a sequence of images that derive from Sumba textiles dating to about 1850–1930 (figs. 5a–i). Figure 5a shows the horse from belt No. 15, where it is a barely discernible scallop on a multicolored ground crowded with other patterns. Figures 5b–h, drawn from *lau pahudu* Nos. 7 and 8, illustrate bipeds and quadrupeds —short, stretched, and prickly spined—all interpreted on Sumba as horses because they have manes, tails, and split jaws. In the original prototype trade textiles, these were probably creatures of several kinds. The repeating sequences of horses (fig. 5h) and of lizards on the far right bands of Nos. 7 and 8, respectively, may derive from a common source: rhythm, curve, and number of repeats are similar, and horse mane and tail correspond to lizard legs. In figure 5i, from a later

version of elephant *lau* No. 7 but based on a similar *pahudu*, the horse identity is unequivocal: no longer stacked in mirrored pairs, naturalistic horses prance upright in a row, all memory of the old alliterative symmetry vanished.

These belts are patterned in a floating weft technique rarely seen in Sumba textiles. Design wefts are completely concealed on the reverse by the warps of the ground weave, which looks unpatterned and plainwoven. Sumbanese employed this technique to fashion belts, pouches, and anklets on a special narrow loom. Single-faced supplementary weft weaving occurs also in north Lampung on certain women's ceremonial skirts[1] and jackets.

1. Tillmann 1938b, plate 23; Maxwell 1990, chapter 3 (Australian National Gallery, Canberra, acc. no. 1987.2459).

Detail, No. 15

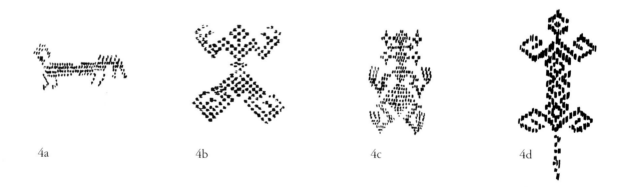

4a   4b   4c   4d

Fig. 4. Details from Sumba belt No. 15

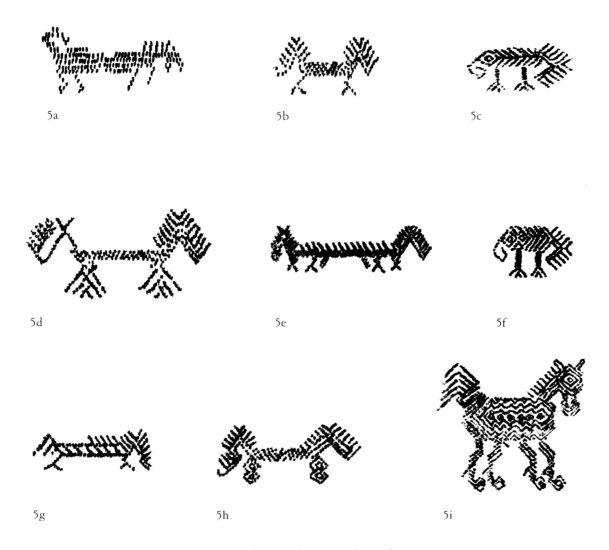

5a

5b

5c

5d

5e

5f

5g

5h

5i

Fig. 5. Horse motifs on Sumba textiles dating from ca. 1850–1930

17. *HINGGI* (MAN'S MANTLE OR HIP CLOTH)
East Sumba
ca. 1920
Cotton; warp ikat
224 × 121 cm (88 × 48 in.) [↕]

Ex-collection: F. Blok, "Boeatan," The Hague

Ancestral male figures stand in urgent frontal pose, with fertile blossoming trees at their loins and crescent-shaped gold chest ornaments above their fingertips. A lavish central geometric pattern is borrowed intact from Indian silk *patola*. Skull trees and roosters rise vertically in the sidebands of the midsection.

Skull-tree imagery is unique to east Sumba. Before the Dutch suppressed Sumba clan warfare (1904–11), headhunting was crucial to the spiritual health of communities. Returning warriors arrayed cut trees with trophy heads "stripped of flesh. . . . Heads [and] lower jaws were hung on a dead tree that stood before the Great House."[1] Skull trees were denuded of bark and implanted in bare rock so that natural growth could never revive; the blood-offering of impaled heads ("fruits") fertilized the community. Headhunting, once widespread in the archipelago, was practiced by all cultures discussed in this catalogue, and served many essential purposes. Spilt blood ensured that crops flourished, and that spirits were appeased ("fed" with scalps and heads lest they strike those at home or cause sickness). Successful headhunting might constitute, among other things, a test of bravery or innocence, an offering to the spirits at building consecrations or rank-raising ceremonies, or an act of vengeance.[2] The prowess of a slain enemy accrued to the hunter. In headhunting, a never-ending divine struggle—between upper and lower worlds, good and evil, growth and decline—was reenacted by man.[3]

The palette and pattern of *hinggi* announced a man's station. Lower classes wore blue and white, aristocrats added red (ritually dyed by women, out of men's sight[4]), and with it black (blue overdyed with red). The high-born merited a fifth color, golden brown. The use of certain motifs, derived for example from *patola*, was the prerogative of particular aristocrats or clans. "One expression

used to denote the nobility. . . in ritual speech is *hundarangga, ru patola*, which comprises the names of especially fine imported silk cloths, originally from India, which are now possessed almost exclusively by the nobles."[5]

Hinggi are designed to function in both present and future. They are worn in identical pairs during a man's lifetime, folded at the shoulder and wrapped about the hips; in death they enshroud him. Individual design elements perform practical functions, and aid the deceased in his journey to the next world. Images of chickens or deer ensure sustenance, horses provide transport, *patola* patterns announce rank, and so forth. Princes were literally mummified in scores of *hinggi*, topped by a silk *patola*.[6] Protected by textiles, a corpse might await burial for twenty years, until relatives could amass the burial goods required for an appropriate funeral and the wealth to provide for guests.[7] The expenditure was staggering.

> For such an occasion, the prince comes with a party of 100 or 150 and stays two months. They eat up everything. . . . No fruit or coconut remains on the trees. . . . Gold jewelry is stuffed in between the layers of textiles wrapped around the corpse and also placed in a separate box which is laid in the grave. The grave may be lined with stacks of gold coins. . . . Dancers, singers, riders, priests, and weavers [are trained]. . . . After the burial, the deceased's favorite horse, [300] buffalo, and horses are stabbed to death and left to die. [Their] flesh may not be eaten. . . . A number of slaves were also killed to make the way to the upper world, build a house, and perform services there. . . . Persons accused of causing the death by witchcraft are killed, their houses destroyed; their women, children, and all their possessions are seized. . . .[8]

1. Adams 1969, p. 13.
2. Downs 1956, pp. 32, 58–67, 56.
3. Downs 1955 presents broad conclusions about headhunting in Indonesia.
4. Adams 1969, p. 75.
5. Forth 1981, p. 463 note 17.
6. Adams 1966, fig. 8.
7. Adams 1969, p. 166.
8. Ibid., pp. 63–68.

TORAJA

18, 19. TWO *MAWA'* (RITUAL CLOTHS)

    18. Seko Lemo (highlands between Galumpang
        and Rongkong), Toraja, central Celebes
        Late 19th century
        Cotton; direct painted
        229 × 66 cm (90 × 26 in.) [↔]

        Exhibited: "Splendid Symbols: Textiles and
        Tradition in Indonesia," Textile Museum,
        Washington, D.C., 1979.
        Published: Gittinger 1979, p. 203; Gittinger
        1980, p. 123.

    19. Sa'dan (?) Toraja, south-central Celebes
        Probably early 19th century
        Cotton; resist-dyed (batik)
        246 × 42 cm (97 × 16½ in.) [↔]

Mawa' (or *maa'*) are the cloths most sacred to the Sa'dan Toraja people.[1] Their supreme deity, Puang Matua, presides in the upperworld within an enclosure curtained with *mawa'*. Toraja chants tell of *mawa'* cloths that originated in heaven long ago and were bestowed by the gods, or brought to man by ancestors who descended from heaven to earth.[2]

And [divine ancestor] Laungku said:[3]
"I am going to enter into a marriage in the edge of the field,
I shall unite myself with the richness of the earth.
"When I have reached maturity, when my form has developed fully,
then shall I rise on high and bear fruit, like the clouds,
then I shall shoot upwards and have flowers, like the white mists.
"Then shall I be spun, like the threads of a cobweb,
then I shall be drawn out, like hairs.
"I shall be made into a *sarita to lamban* with a design of men fording a river,
I shall become a *maa'* with a pattern of swimming men.
"I shall be made into a *doti langi'* with a cross motif on it,
I shall become a *maa'* to whose folding up there is no end.
"Then shall I lie in a basket adorned with a design, cherishing all the precious things put therein with me,
then I shall lie in a carrying hamper on which a wave-shaped pattern is cut, protecting the property that is there with me."[4]

Mawa' sanctify every important Sa'dan ritual, after being ceremoniously removed from their storage place high in the rafters of the home and "kissed" with the breath of a woman.[5] In their manifold uses, they seem to represent a special divine grace bestowed upon particular persons and places. *Mawa'* crown the heads of young virgins who, in the Bua' purification feast, ritually wed mankind to heaven; they canopy and cushion the sedan chair in which these young women, swathed head to toe also in *mawa'*, are paraded aloft, stiff as wooden dolls.[6] *Mawa'* hang from fences to delimit ceremonial compounds, and cover the drums whose beat drives evil away.[7] Priests wear them as headcloths at Merok feasts of thanksgiving.[8] During great Toraja death rituals, *mawa'* enshroud the corpse and drape both the bier and the sacrificial buffalo that will transport the deceased to the afterworld.[9] *Mawa'* adorn altars and sanctify the ancestral house of the deceased's clan.[10] They have the power to bless man, his crops, and his livestock with health and fortune, and to ward off disease.[11] *Mawa'* are the "umbilical cord" of great men, and *sarita* (No. 20) the placenta.[12] Each *mawa'* is known by a personal name and possesses specific powers.[13]

    Mawa' occur in several distinct visual styles, but the design is always painted, dyed, or printed. Most are actually old Indian chintz, which arrived in Celebes as one component of spice trade exchange and were passed to interior Celebes via coastal Bugis peoples.[14] Occasionally, these chintz retain very old features: for example, images of dancing girls with "floating eyes"[15] (an iconographic feature that disappeared from painting at the Indian source in the early sixteenth century), or color, design, and texture nearly identical to Indian chintz fragments of the fifteenth to eighteenth century preserved in Fustat, Egypt.[16] Toraja's preference for these archaic types signifies a long-standing Indian connection. Indian chintz found in Toraja corresponds in dimension to costly silk *patola*, and may at some historical juncture have become a cheaper substitute for them. A small subgroup of *mawa'* appears to be old Javanese batik, perhaps manufactured at moments when trade in Indian goods was interrupted.

    The most compelling *mawa'*, however, are the rare autochthonous pieces made long ago, in which no connection to Indian design is evident. Their imagery reflects Toraja ritual themes and stylistic vocabulary (Indian chintz are iconographically irrelevant to Toraja). Modest in dimension and usually made of homespun cotton, they have a palette of smoky black and buff; the

18

technique is either direct painted as in No. 18, or rough batik as in No. 19.[17]

In *mawa'* No. 18, men stand with limbs flexed and fingers splayed in a metaphorical landscape: cruciform motifs, which carry the association of abundance, evoke a plain of plenty through which the buffalo pass to a sacred corral. *Mawa'* with crosses are known as *doti langi'*, "spots of heaven," the name of the pattern on the cloth that veils Puang Matua, the supreme deity, in heaven.[18]

Buffalo are the preeminent sacrificial animal in Toraja, the source of prestige and the measure by which other wealth is gauged. At death feasts, the deceased is identified with a buffalo, which carries the soul to the hereafter and guards the dead.[19] Feast givers strive to surpass one another in the number and size of the buffalo they offer for sacrifice. Enormous horn spans are especially prized; Toraja pictorial art flaunts that breadth by tilting the animals' heads ninety degrees.

Earthy brown-black *mawa'*, such as No. 19, depict elements at the heart of village well-being, disposed naturalistically within a real space. Here, buffalo file through a landscape, with their suckling young. Two sway-backed Toraja houses or rice barns on stilts dominate the center of the scene. Human figures stand between these structures, pounding rice in a canoe-shaped wooden mortar. Roosters strut on the rooftops.[20] Other dark-dyed *mawa'* depict pigs, dogs, riders on horseback, and women weaving at backstrap looms. All have dotted or striated backgrounds.

Images on Bronze Age kettledrums probably made on the Southeast Asian mainland and dating from approximately the second century B.C. to the third century A.D. suggest interesting parallels. One such drum excavated on Sangeang Island off south Celebes (fig. 6) shows horsemen, livestock, rice pounders, and saddle-roofed houses raised on stilts—aspects of village life identical to those depicted on dark *mawa'*—similarly delineated and arranged in an elongated horizontal format. The drum's gouged metal background has a pebbly, dotted surface that resembles the visual texture

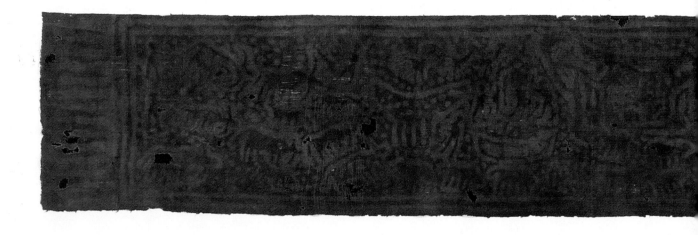

19

of these *mawa'*. Such resemblance to "black" *mawa'* imagery, presentation, and detail suggests a direct continuity of vision from ancient times, far more pertinent to Toraja culture than the Indian iconography of the ornate chintz also known as *mawa'* in Toraja.

Subtle color contrast and diffuse batik line lend "black" *mawa'* an oddly beguiling, haunting quality; people and animals drift through space like specters. Dreamlike visions of prosperity are among the invocations of the Merok feast, as the chief of ritual invites the gods to come to his village clan house:

> As sustenance for the journey, take the sow, which
> farrows plentifully, as provisions on the way, take the
> swine that drop young, which roam far and wide.
> As sustenance for the journey, take the fowls, sitting on
> their perches, as provisions on the way, take the claws
> that are trimmed with a small knife.
> As sustenance for the journey, take the *sarita* with the
> design of men fording a river, as provisions on the
> way, take the *maa'* with the pattern of swimming
> men.
> As sustenance for the journey, take the gold *keris* [dagger]
> of great size, as provisions on the way, take the
> *kandaure* [beadwork] with the cords hanging low.
> All the goods of all kinds, all the possessions together.
> An auspicious dream, a pregnant nocturnal vision.
> A countenance full of goodwill, a benevolent
> appearance, riches in quantity, like foliage; precious
> things, like the branches of the tree.
> Everything that will be in their thoughts, all the things
> of which they are mindful.[21]

1. Early published data concerning the central weaving districts between Rongkong and Galumpang, where virtually all Toraja material in this catalogue was made, is scant. However, the north (Palu and Poso) and south (Sa'dan) Toraja districts have been extensively studied, and comparison of these regions suggests that many general beliefs and practices were shared throughout Toraja.
2. Nooy-Palm 1980, pp. 83, 84.
3. Laungku, father of cotton, was the third of eight siblings created from divine bellows. Datu Laukku', ancestress of the Toraja, was the first. The others created poison, rain, fowl, buffalo, iron, and rice.
4. Van der Veen 1965, pp. 92, 93.
5. Nooy-Palm 1979, p. 257.
6. Nooy-Palm 1986, pp. 12, 43.
7. Van der Veen 1965, p. 8; Nooy-Palm 1986, pp. 75, 79.
8. Nooy-Palm 1986, pp. 73, 77, 83; Van der Veen 1965, p. 7.
9. Nooy-Palm 1979, p. 258; Nooy-Palm 1980, pp. 89, 93.
10. Nooy-Palm 1980, p. 89; Nooy-Palm 1986, p. 82.
11. Nooy-Palm 1980, p. 85.
12. Van der Veen 1966, p. 29.
13. Nooy-Palm 1980, p. 85.
14. Ibid., p. 92, fig. 3, exemplifies very late *mawa'*.
15. Guy 1987, figs. 7–9.
16. Yoshioka and Yoshimoto 1980, plates 85, 86, illustrates examples of this type found in Toraja.
17. An additional stamped and painted type of *mawa'*, with garish red and aqua chemical tints, was made until recently in Sa'dan Toraja.
18. Nooy-Palm 1970, p. 187; Nooy-Palm 1980, p. 91 note 4.
19. Nooy-Palm 1979, p. 198.
20. Roosters are associated with man and sacrificed at rituals. The Judge in the Kingdom of the Dead is Pong Lalondong (*londong*, "cock"). Nooy-Palm 1979, p. 211.
21. Van der Veen 1965, p. 65.

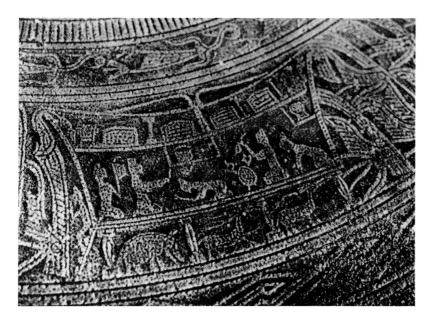

Fig. 6. Detail of pattern on ancient bronze kettledrum found on Sangeang,
central Indonesia. After Bernet Kempers, *The Kettledrums of Southeast Asia* (1988),
plate 4.02f

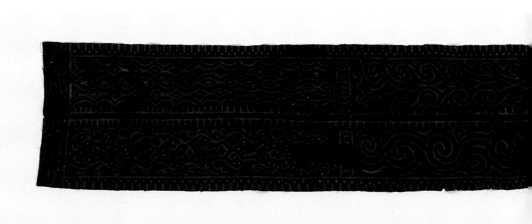

20. *SARITA* (BANNER OR WRAP)

Sa'dan (?) Toraja, south-central Celebes
19th century
Cotton; resist-dyed
267 × 30 cm (105 × 12 in.) [↔]

Sarita, like *mawa'*, are cloths sacred to the Sa'dan Toraja. Long and narrow, they are worn by important people, wrapped around the head or across the chest, during rituals and feasts. They encircle groups of special celebrants. They are folded and placed upon the dead or draped around wooden death effigies (*tau-tau*). Ribbon-like, they hang from the gables of the clan house. They link the clan to offerings to the gods: one end of the *sarita* fastens to the *petua* ("bearers of life") housepoles of the clan house, the other to the tree beside which buffalo are sacrificed.[1]

Most *sarita* are imported, though not all their places of manufacture have been identified. Patterned (like Toraja carved house façades) with successive passages of abstract design, they are resist-dyed indigo on natural buff.[2] The rare Toraja-made batiked *sarita*, however, are black; and like dark *mawa'*, their iconography parallels that of ancient Bronze Age artifacts.[3] The deer and tiger cats depicted on this *sarita* are similar to those on the Sangeang drum noted in No. 19.[4] Likewise, figures appear in profile within long rectangular scenes. Swirling meanders suggest the bands that often decorate early bronzes (fig. 7). Spoked sun disks recall the ubiquitous central motif of drum tympana.

1. Van der Veen 1965, p. 6; Nooy-Palm 1980, pp. 89, 90, and fig. 5.
2. Solyom 1984, p. ii.
3. One other fine black *sarita* is published; Gittinger 1979, p. 202.
4. Bernet Kempers 1988, plates 4.02i–k.

Fig. 7. Detail from the "Moon of Bali," a bronze kettledrum found at Pejeng, Bali. After Bernet Kempers, *The Kettledrums of Southeast Asia* (1988), plate 3.01c

**21, 22. TWO *PEWO* (OR *MBESA TALI TO BATU*)
(HEADWRAPPERS OR LOINCLOTHS)**

Rongkong (or Palu?) Toraja, central Celebes
Acquired in Palu River districts
ca. 1850–1900
Cotton; discontinuous retracing wefts forming
openwork patterns, tie-dyed after weaving

21. 419 × 36 cm (165 × 14 in.) [↕]

22. 496 × 33 cm (195 ½ × 13 in.) [↕]

Technique occasionally projects such a strong presence
that it defines the essence of a piece. *Pewo* were woven
uncolored, with a complex and ever-changing network of
tiny slits which predetermined the pattern that would
emerge when the fabrics were later dyed (fig. 8). After
weaving, small sections of fabric were wrapped and
tightly bound between the slits; these areas remained
protected ("reserved") while the entire textile was plunged
into the dye bath. The bundles were then cut open and
other portions retied for the next color bath.[1] The
resulting effect is a soft, shimmering staccato.

Typically, *pewo* are organized in sequences of patterned compartments—the same archaic arrangement
favored in blue-and-white *sarita*, cardwoven bands, *roto*
(No. 23), and *porilonjong* (No. 24), and also characteristic of other Toraja decorated arts. The interplay of
monumental and delicate passages creates rhythmic
richness. No. 22 deviates from this norm in the continuous sweep of its design. Both Nos. 21 and 22 are
exceptionally long, meticulously woven, and deeply
dyed.

Pewo were used in death rituals. According to data
obtained between 1922 and 1939 by Jaap and Laurens
Langewis, "with the deceased raised to a sitting position,
one of his closest blood relations wound [*pewo*] around
his head, and then conducted him to interment."[2] A
north Toraja name for these remarkable cloths is *mbesa tali
to batu*, "headcloth of the stone man"[3] (possibly referring
to the megalithic stone sculptures of human figures in
Palu). Kruyt identifies *pewo* as loincloths used only in
mountain districts.[4] In Rongkong, allegedly a place of
pewo manufacture, *pewo* weaving technique is called
tannunan dasi, "sewn or needlework weaving"; "sewing"
of supplementary weft yarns was performed on the loom
with a bamboo needle. Despite the early attribution of
one *pewo* to Rongkong district, southeast Toraja,[5] all
recently found examples have emerged from the north
Palu district, which supports our supposition that Palu,

in addition to Rongkong and Galumpang, was a separate
Toraja weaving center (see text, No. 28).

Although a similar weaving technique occurs in
banana fiber on Sangir Island north of Celebes, and many
fascinating forms of kilim and tapestry weave have
recently come to light in Sumatra, Malaya, Bali, and
Lombok, no other Indonesian textiles are ikatted *after*
weaving in this singular, archaic manner.

1. For an account of *pewo* manufacture, see Jager Gerlings 1952, pp.
    40–43. Sa'dan Toraja *pote* (widows' hoods) are technically related
    (see Nooy-Palm 1975, pp. 65–66); a fine *pote* is published in
    Solyom 1984, fig. 65.
2. Jager Gerlings 1952, p. 40.
3. Kruyt 1938, vol. 3, p. 508.
4. Ibid., vol. 4, p. 248.
5. Jager Gerlings 1952, p. 40. *Pewo* were not, however, recognized
    as a local production by Rongkong villagers during visits in 1974
    and 1975.

Detail, No. 21

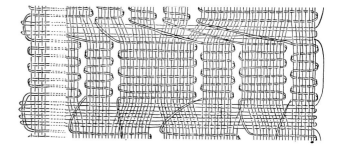

Fig. 8. Diagram of *pewo* weaving. After Jager Gerlings,
Sprekende weefsels (1952), fig. 10

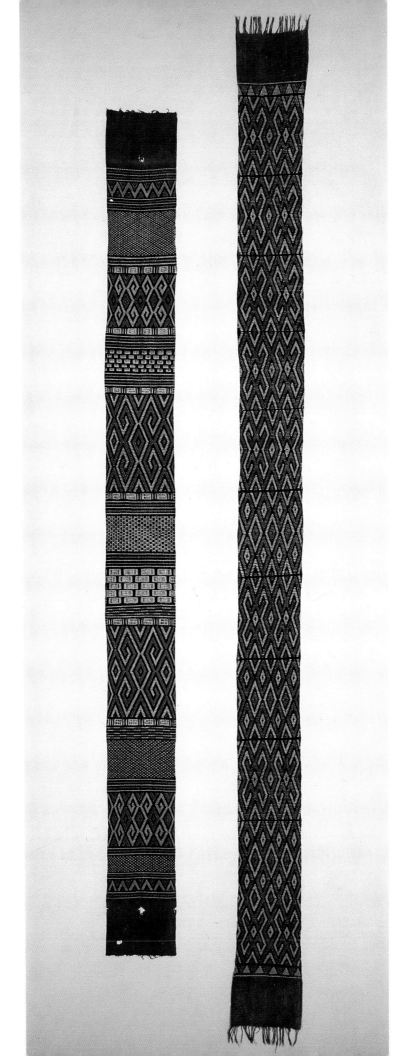

23. *ROTO* (FESTIVAL BANNER)

Rongkong Toraja, central Celebes
Probably late 19th century
Cotton; pelangi
409 × 49 cm (161 × 19½ in.) [↕]

Pelangi (meaning "rainbow") is a widely practiced technique in the western and central Malay Archipelago. Portions of fabric are gathered and tied, usually with fiber, to resist the dye. Refined pelangi technique on silk results in florals, meanders, and dainty stars within courtly framed formats (Palembang, east-coastal Sumatra), crazy-quilt splashes of garish color (Bali and Java), or somber, rich diamond-patterned shawls with a gauzy hypnotic presence (Gresik, made for the central Javanese courts). Softly glowing cotton pelangi reflect an earlier tradition, best seen on Sasak textiles from Lombok, which more closely approach the sensibility of Toraja *roto* such as this one.

Local informants speak of *roto* designs as representations of the sun and constellations. Many flamboyant *roto*—twenty feet or more in length, with vivid color on tight weave—have bands of tie-dyed rings contrasting in scale and conformation that evoke stars.[1] The present example is more subdued. Homespun, gauzy, and resonant, it bears an uncanny resemblance to tie-dyed textiles from ancient Peru.[2]

1.   Khan Majlis 1984, nineteenth color plate following page 160.
2.   Van Nouhuys 1925, p. 122.

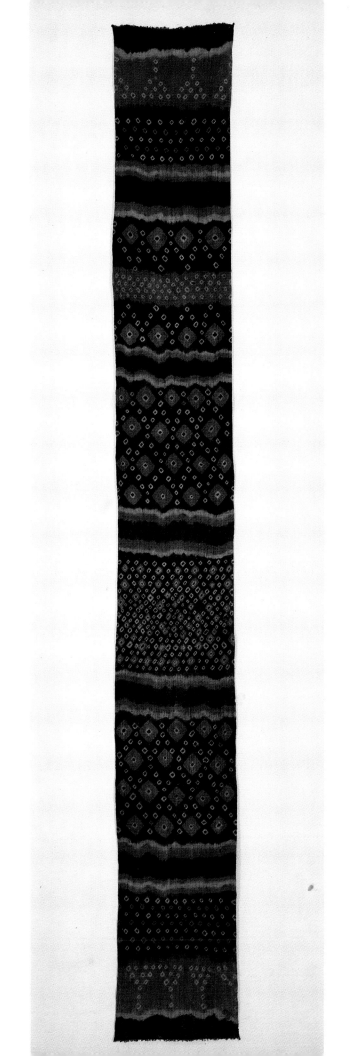

24. *PORILONJONG* (CEREMONIAL HANGING)

Rongkong or Mamasa Toraja, central Celebes
ca. 1900–15
Cotton; warp ikat
491×154 cm (193½×60½ in.) [↕]

Ex-collection: G. H. R. von Koenigswald, Bad
    Homburg
Exhibited: "Indonesië-Oceanië," Museum voor
    Land-en Volkenkunde, Rotterdam, 1965.
Published: Rotterdam 1965, figs. 12, 13 (no. 40).

Old Toraja ikats rarely present figural imagery. Enormous ceremonial hangings called *porilonjong* typically display a centerfield of successive geometric bands. This singular *porilonjong*, however, depicts crocodiles and deer, which may represent clan totems. Crocodiles actually lurk in Rongkong and Galumpang rivers. When "Bad Luck" haunts travelers, crocodiles may seize them; but crocodiles can also transport men back from the underworld and from death itself.[1] The ambivalent role of this creature is expressed even more sharply in the Palu Toraja belief that when a woman gives birth to twins, one twin may be human, the other crocodilian (see also the shadowy crocodile "companions" on Sumba *lau hada* No. 2). Descendants of the human twin will never be harmed by crocodiles.[2] Some Palu Toraja believe that their ancestors were deer.[3] Perhaps the clan that made and used the present *porilonjong* claimed crocodile or deer founders. Crocodiles of similar shape appear in relief alongside Dongsonian masks and birds on large protohistoric megalithic vats found in north Toraja.[4]

Above and below these crocodiles, "dancing deer" appear; their angular backs, long whip tails, and the curly tendrils against a fragmented ground suggest links with a group of very old (eighteenth century or earlier) Indonesian cotton weft ikats recently discovered among ethnic Lampungers in Komering district, south Sumatra (fig. 9).[5] These Komering ikats—delicately patterned on astonishingly fine cotton filaments—assemble in one tightly integrated design field a large number of patterns featured separately on later weavings throughout the archipelago (Borneo *pua*, Balinese *geringsing* and *cepuk*, Toraja ikats).[6] Such Komering cloths are probably quite close in appearance to a trade textile no longer extant but once widely circulated that may have been the source of the unusual deer depiction in this *porilonjong*.

The soft yarn, somewhat loose weave, and little ribbonlike white-on-red meanders of this cloth are characteristic of Rongkong textiles. The very length of

porilonjong represents an extraordinary technical achievement. The weaver had to maintain precise alignment of yarns over a long span for repeated tie-and-dye, and then by body pressure alone sustain even warp tension while weaving on an elementary backstrap loom.[7]

In Rongkong, *porilonjong* were hung horizontally on fences to delimit and protect a ritually sacred area; in Sa'dan, they were hung along the walls during death rituals.[8] Field photographs show Toraja ikats of similar dimension (*rindulolo*) surrounding a Sa'dan death house and held aloft to canopy a row of Palu dancers.[9] An old man in Rongkong told us that on the day after a ceremony, displayed cloths were washed and then laid out on the ground to dry, so numerous that they "shut out the sun."

The companion piece to this *porilonjong* at the Honolulu Academy of Arts, which was tied and dyed together with it, was reportedly acquired in Mamasa district, southwest Toraja.[10] Ikat rarely occurs in pairs in Toraja.

1. Kruyt 1938, vol. 4, p. 350; vol. 3, p. 555.
2. Ibid., vol. 3, pp. 170–71.
3. Ibid., vol. 1, p. 298.
4. Ibid., vol. 5, figs. 108, 109.
5. One Komering ikat is illustrated in Holmgren and Spertus 1989a; the genre is thoroughly catalogued in Holmgren et al. 1991.
6. Holmgren and Spertus 1989a.
7. Bezemer n.d., fig. 19, an early photograph of a Toraja woman seated on the ground, weaving a *porilonjong* on a backstrap loom, with warps stretching high up among the house beams.
8. Nooy-Palm 1975, p. 76.
9. Nooy-Palm 1986, p. 219; Kruyt 1938, vol. 5, fig. 43.
10. Honolulu Academy of Arts 1989, acc. no. 5100.1.

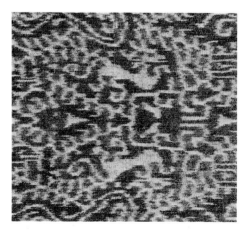

Fig. 9. Detail (actual size) of a cotton weft ikat from Komering, south Sumatra. Collection Anita E. Spertus and Robert J. Holmgren

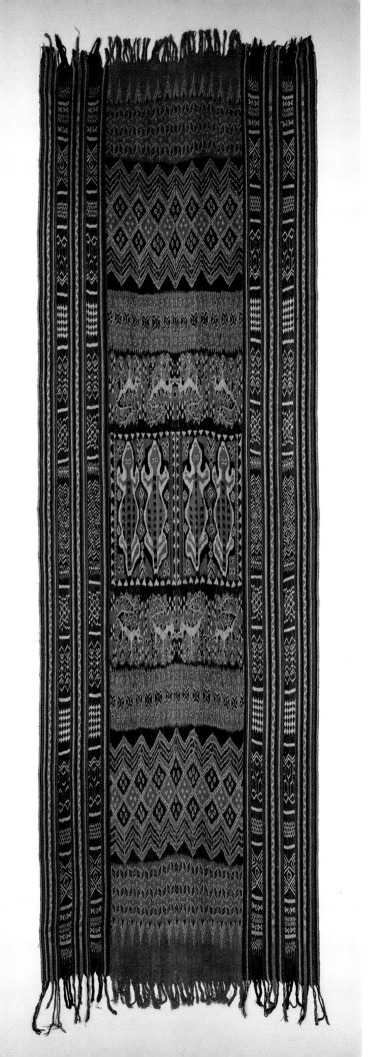

25. *SEKOMANDI* (FUNERAL SHROUD)

Galumpang (Mangki) Toraja, central Celebes
Late 19th century
Cotton; warp ikat
171×264 cm (67½×104 in.) [↕]

Like a modern color-field painting, this textile projects steady metric energy. Arrows course up and down within its space. Positive and negative interact with equal force—a controlled dynamism. Pattern seems to generate endlessly, as if the borders of the cloth serve to frame, or "window," a vast unseen plain beyond (windowing is a common visual device in Toraja). Lyrical side stripes (the *kaki*, or "feet," of the textile) vary in width and hue, relaxing the central tension and allowing it to breathe. Brick-red color, yarn with a hard burnished surface, and tight weave are unique to Galumpang ikat.

In both Rongkong and Galumpang, ikats were used as ceremonial hangings and shrouds, not as clothing (see text, No. 28). "A special industry practiced in the Galumpang area . . . is the weaving of the so-called *kain sekumandi* or shroud, in fine sober colors and artistic decoration. Every self-respecting resident of Galumpang possesses such a shroud in his lifetime, to serve upon his death."[1]

The pioneer comparative ethnographer Carl Schuster identified metrically repetitive patterns like those seen here as "genealogical patterns . . . best understood as representing (or as having represented originally) a

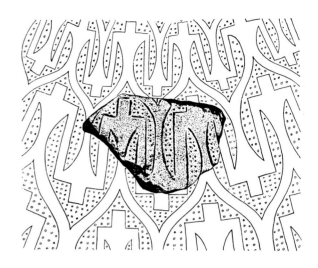

Fig. 11. Pattern of interlocking human figures on an ancient potsherd unearthed in Galumpang, central Celebes, extended and reconstructed in diagram by Carl Schuster. After Van Heekeren, *The Stone Age of Indonesia* (1972), fig. 46

succession of deceased ancestors, whose arrangement in connected series provides an image of the social fabric." With characteristic daring, Schuster traced "genealogical patterns" back to the sixth millennium B.C., "and its origin probably lies still further back in time."[2] Applying Schuster's theory, Jager Gerlings extracted individual *sekomandi* design elements from a densely patterned context, to view them in isolation: recurrent human figures emerge, one standing above the other, and linked to adjacent figures at the leg, rightside up and upside down (fig. 10).[3] Ancient pottery fragments unearthed in the same Galumpang locale and dated variously from 200 B.C. to A.D. 1400 by different authorities[4] depict an analogous net of interlocking figures (fig. 11), their heads and torsos more clearly human in shape than those on *sekomandi*.

The community of ancestors in the afterlife mitigates the finality of death; entrance into their fellowship is an honor. In Schuster's interpretation, ancestors are shown gathered on a shroud such as this one to accompany the deceased to his orderly place in the next world.

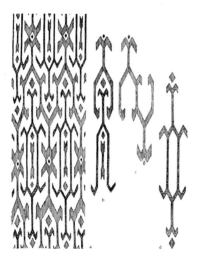

Fig. 10. Carl Schuster's interpretation of a *sekomandi* pattern as an interlocked network of human figures. After Jager Gerlings, *Sprekende Weefsels* (1952), fig. 27

1. Schuster 1965, caption to plate 88, quoting J. F. W. L. Goslings, "De Toradja's van Galoempang," *Kolonial Tijdschrift* (Amsterdam) 22 (1933), p. 75.
2. Schuster 1965, pp. 342–43.
3. Jager Gerlings 1952, p. 120.
4. Schuster 1965, p. 345 note 6.

26.   *PAPORITONOLING* (CEREMONIAL
        WEAVING)

Galumpang Toraja, west-central Celebes
Second half of the 19th century
Cotton; warp ikat
165 × 127 cm (65 × 50 in.) [↕]

Ikats allegedly woven in the now-abandoned village of
Tonoling[1] are the most stunning Toraja textiles—a
unique class of consistently satisfying masterworks.
Whereas most Toraja ikats from the Galumpang area
conform to three or four pattern types (No. 25 is a
representative example), no two *paporitonoling* are the
same. They may have served a special function. Approximately thirty-five such ikats are known worldwide.

     Big complex repeating patterns, a balanced mingling
of large and small emblems, and stark color contrasts
invest *paporitonoling* with unexpected energy and power.
In No. 26, four giant *sekongs* (flexed four-armed shapes),
which Toraja interpret as squatting ancestral anthropomorphs, are packed with little cruciform motifs that
evoke abundance (see text, No. 18). Sharp red points leap
from the *sekong* perimeters like small flames, answered in
perfect proportion by the black dentation of the ground.
Asymmetric borders, and small crosses and dots freely
scattered on the ground, impart a bright, spontaneous air.

1.   According to several local informants, Tonoling was reportedly
      situated on the north bank of the Karama River, opposite the
      modern district administration town of Galumpang, which
      replaced it around the turn of this century. One textile of the
      present genre type was acquired by Van Nouhuys from "Kurawak"
      (possibly Kalawak village, now abandoned, in the Karataun
      valley, Galumpang). Van Nouhuys 1925, p. 117.

27.   *PAPORITONOLING* (CEREMONIAL
        WEAVING)

Galumpang Toraja, west-central Celebes
18th or early 19th century
165 × 138 cm (65 × 54½ in.) [↕]

No. 27 is the earliest example of the *paporitonoling* genre
known to us, based on its supple forms, large dotted
and feathery *tumpal* (triangular) borders, and color. It is
clearly *patola*-derived. The dominant central emblems
relate directly to the distinctive four-lobed *habaku* designs often seen on *patola* centerfields in Sumba ikat
hinggi;[1] the *paporitonoling*'s toothy notched surrounds
correspond to the twisting tendrils of early Sumba
patola-based patterns (e.g., No. 11) despite striking dis-
parities of scale, technique, and impression. The red
ground and shades of turquoise approximate color tones
of the oldest Gujarati *patola* found in Indonesia.[2] However, this cloth—angular, strong, exploded in scale,
with tickling cilia-lined perimeters and sprinkles of
dots—expresses a dynamism entirely different from that
of the precious jewellike *patola* silks that inspired it.

1.   Langewis and Wagner 1964, plate 24.
2.   Holmgren and Spertus 1989b.

28. CEREMONIAL SARONG (*PORITUTU?*)

Palu or Galumpang Toraja, central Celebes
19th century
Cotton; warp ikat
154 × 195 cm (60½ × 77 in.) [↕]

Palu peoples live in villages clustered mainly along tributaries of the Palu River in northwest Toraja. According to local legend, the land was once the site of an important culture; stone megaliths, including monumental ancestor figures, lend some credence to this claim. In Southeast Asia, similar monoliths are found in Pasemah-Lampung (south Sumatra) and central Laos. The persistent and notably sacramental use in Palu of barkcloth, a precursor of weaving and probably made for thousands of years in Indonesia, signals that ties to ancient times were still very strong into the twentieth century.[1]

Although Palu was studied in depth during the period 1890–1930,[2] Palu ikat weaving virtually escaped notice—an odd oversight, because textiles found in Palu and neighboring Poso include the oldest and most refined in Toraja. Local ikat production apparently stopped before European ethnographers arrived at the end of the nineteenth century.[3] Because they saw no cloths being made locally and new cloths arriving in trade from Rongkong, they must have assumed that the old textiles in use in Palu had also been made elsewhere. Indeed, early twentieth-century photographs,[4] statements by local informants, and present-day dispersion patterns indicate that both the Rongkong and Galumpang Toraja did sell or trade many ikats to Palu and Poso Toraja in the north. There they were used not as shrouds (as in the south) but as sarongs, supplanting the traditional voluminous brown barkcloth skirts. Folded, ikats also functioned as ceremonial seats.[5] Rongkong and Galumpang textiles intended for northern trade bear distinctive patterns,[6] which may have simulated the local production they replaced.

A group of apparently indigenous early cloths has emerged from Palu and Poso in recent years that preserves features of extremely old Indonesian weaving evident elsewhere in the archipelago: sequences of narrow weft stripes that deepen in hue every few threads, then alternate with ikat bands;[7] warp ikats that clearly recall plaiting patterns; or emblems in sequential squares similar to rare old Bentenan ikats from the northern tip of Celebes.[8]

The present sarong is probably a true Palu weaving. Although tightly woven like Galumpang cloths and similar in pattern to well-known Rongkong *porisitutu',*[9] its overall sensibility points to a unique provenance and approach: a singing, rhythmically varied quality characterized by syncopated border-pattern colors, *tumpals* that closely mimic Indian chintz, distinctive shades of cherry red and turquoise, abbreviated *kakis* (striped outer panels) with minute "zippers," color-variegated chain patterns, and a humming central *sekong* pattern that seems to extend endlessly.

1. For Toraja barkcloth, see Gittinger 1979, no. 164a,b; Kaudern 1944, plates I–LVII; Kooijman 1963, plates VIII–XI, XXI–XXVII.
2. Important works about the north Toraja are those by Kruyt and Adriani (especially 1938), Grubauer 1923, Kaudern 1944, and the Sarasin brothers (1905).
3. By analogy fine bronze casting had recently died out; Kaudern 1944, pp. 308–10.
4. E.g., Kruyt 1938, vol. 5, figs. 38, 39, 47, 145, 146, 183, 246.
5. Ibid., vol. 3, p. 329; on page 507, Kruyt ascribes a Rongkong provenance to these ikats.
6. Van Nouhuys 1921, plates 3–5.
7. Khan Majlis 1984, color plate opposite page 161. Compare ikats from Sasak areas (Lombok; ibid., p. 78), Sembiran (central Bali), and Komering (north Lampung; Holmgren and Spertus 1989a, and Holmgren et al. 1991).
8. Khan Majlis 1984, eighteenth color plate following page 160; Kartiwa 1987, pp. 47, 62.
9. The variant spellings of this word are regional. For a Rongkong *porisitutu',* see Langewis and Wagner 1964, no. 29.

LAMPUNG

29–32. FOUR *TAMPAN* (RITUAL WEAVINGS)

Pasisir (coastal) peoples, south coast of Lampung
19th century
Cotton; supplementary weft

29. Punduh, Lampung Bay
73 × 72 cm (28½ × 28½ in.) [↕]
Published: Holmgren and Spertus 1980,
fig. 18.

30. Piya, Wai Ratai, Lampung Bay
79 × 73 cm (31 × 28½ in.) [↕]
Exhibited: "Splendid Symbols: Textiles and
Tradition in Indonesia," Textile Museum,
Washington, D.C., 1979.
Published: Gittinger 1979, no. 55; Holmgren
1979, p. 30; Gittinger 1980, p. 122;
Holmgren and Spertus 1980, fig. 5.

31. Putih Doh, Semangka Bay
69 × 68 cm (27 × 27 in.) [↕]
Published: Holmgren and Spertus 1980,
fig. 8.

32. Hanauberak, Wai Ratai, Lampung Bay
Discontinuous weft openwork, and twining
·93 × 81 cm (36½ × 32 in.) [↕]
Published: Holmgren and Spertus 1980,
fig. 20.

Lampung textiles tantalize with recollections of ancient traditions and beliefs, reflected in dramatic maritime settings and expressed in painterly classical imagery.

Of all Lampung cloths, *tampan* enjoy the widest range of ceremonial use. They are owned by almost every family, and function at the ritual heart of the community. They serve not as clothing or decoration but as tangible assertions and reminders of man's bond to the sacred world. Every transition in individual and societal life entails vulnerability and disruption; *tampan* offer protection, consecrating, stabilizing, and facilitating these passages. At such moments—birth, death, circumcision, marriage, petition, house-raising, and ascendancy in rank, among others—*tampan* become ceremonial seats, pillows for the dead, covers for ritual gifts, protective crowns atop main house-poles, and reliquaries. Their ship imagery evokes a spiritual lifeboat that safely conveys the community, through uncertainties, from one state of stability to another.

Tampan appear in various styles. Those from the mountainous hinterland often display angular abstractions of trees, birds, animals, houses, stacked boats, or simple repetitive rows of geometric designs. *Tampan* of the *pasisir* ("coastal") style, such as those seen here,

however, exhibit articulate painterly tableaux of much greater sophistication.[1]

Dramas unfold in real space, with birds in the sky, a waterline, and sea life swimming in the deep. Narrative scenes are glimpsed as if passing by a window. Figures appear in profile and interact. The stark contrast between dark foreground and light background brings to mind Indonesian *wayang* shadow dramas illuminated from behind. Each scene is imbued with a distinctive atmosphere: the serenity of a barque gliding as if over mirror-smooth waters (No. 29),[2] the breezy openness of sails billowing in the wind (No. 32). Characters perform real functions, such as the pilot in feathered headdress who plumbs the waters to steer his vessel past dangerous shoals (No. 30; in one Borneo society, a spiritual leader wearing a similar headdress guides his community "out of darkness and into light, out of sickness into health, from death into life"[3]). Small manned lifeboats are pulled in readiness behind the mother ships. Costume is described in careful detail (the bustle and drape of court dress on the main figure in No. 31); glossy silk yarns highlight special features (the golden "treasure box," center right in No. 32). A full gamelan orchestra, with players beating drums and gongs, suggests an aural dimension (No. 30). Planes of observation shift to display every image from its most descriptive angle: in No. 30, the crocodile appears in profile (not archaically frontal as in Sumba and Toraja cloths), a crab and turtles are viewed from above. In their approach to compositional balance and harmony, Lampung *pasisir* weavers visualize a profound philosophical objective: to project an ideal image of their society united as a hierarchical collective.

Little is known about the early Lampung culture in which these spellbinding textiles were conceived. The gradual penetration of Islam commencing in the sixteenth century changed Lampung's cultural direction. After 1825, Dutch interference further sapped Lampung's vitality. Visitors before 1900 never described textiles; around that date elaborate *pasisir* weaving (always rare, the sumptuary prerogative of aristocrats) died out. Other material manifestations of early Lampung—such as spirit houses and elaborately decorated architecture—that would help to elucidate iconographic meaning have virtually disappeared. Our knowledge of the culture and its imagery therefore remains largely speculative and based on broad visual and ethnographic parallels with other, better-known societies. Thus, for example, the treelike branched structure supported by two courtiers at

29

left center in No. 30 corresponds to Borneo *sanggaran*, which marked places where animal and human sacrifices were offered during ritual events. The two birds that perch in its topmost boughs may represent, as they do in Borneo, the chief deities of the upperworld and underworld, balanced in philosophical confrontation.[4]

Early scholars interpreted *tampan* vessels as "ships of the dead," in which the souls of the deceased journeyed to the land of their ancestors. In Borneo, important elements of *tampan* iconography—gamelan, *sanggaran*, ships, and trees of life—are in fact associated with mortuary rites, while coffins are shaped like boats.[5] Early colonial sources tell of Indonesian chiefs with large retinues of slaves (substitutes for courtiers) who were buried with their ships at sea.[6] *Tampan* imagery may also illustrate ships on which legendary ancestors journeyed from the upperworld to earth (see text, No. 8). All these speculations, however, probably are subordinate to the essential symbolism of boats as organized communities. In Borneo myth, the earth is called "River of the World";[7] society floats on its waters.

Tampan depict technical devices of ancient ocean-going ships. Southeast Asians were primary carriers of Indian Ocean trade in the first millennium A.D. As early as the third century, a Chinese chronicler marveled at ships, probably Indonesian, that carried hundreds of passengers and large cargoes.[8] *Tampan* such as No. 30 portray vessels that correspond in construction to huge ships made before 1600: elaborate planking in the hull, sails of joined mats, exterior rudders (a steering device distinctive to Indonesia and south Asia), the absence of outriggers (an encumbrance to large ships on the open sea but stabilizing in coastal waters), and multiple decks.

The images of great ships transformed into virtual palace communities (No. 32), the realism, and the fluent iconographic variety of *tampan pasisir*, which stand so dramatically apart from other textile traditions in Indonesia, together suggest that Lampung had a highly cosmopolitan character shaped by maritime exposure to other cultures. Although for several centuries Lampung has been an ignored backwater of little economic or political consequence, there are indications that it had a more important role in precolonial periods. It lay astride the strategic ocean crossroads of the Sunda and Malacca straits—millennia-old funnels for all sea trade between China/Southeast Asia, and India and the West. It adjoined classical Indonesia's twin poles of trade, the Srivijaya empire to the immediate north and Java to the

east. At various times Lampung was absorbed politically within more powerful Sumatran and Javanese overlord states. Situated slightly aside the power center, Lampung could appropriate influences from many corners without being a main target of political attack or subject to abrupt shifts in cultural direction: Lampung was courted as an ally, not crushed as an enemy.

The full sophistication and grandeur documented in *tampan pasisir* blossomed during the precolonial period, when west Indonesians carried shipping and trade to China, India, and beyond, and Indonesian entrepôt states flourished from contact with passing traffic. As a rule, ancient mariners clung to the coasts even on long journeys. Thus, the Strait of Malacca was the passageway of choice from archipelagic waters to the Indian Ocean. Because it is long and narrow, however, and studded with islands, transit there was often disrupted by pirates or hostage to political feuds. When Sumatran states were weakened and powerless to maintain order, use of the alternative Sunda Strait, short and wide, probably increased—and with it, presumably, south Lampung's fortunes. The presence of some of Indonesia's earliest states (Ko-ying, Kan-t'o-li, Tarumanegara) near this latter waterway raises the intriguing possibility that voyages across the open ocean—monsoon winds could have swept ships directly from Indonesia to the east coast of Africa—were undertaken in the early first millennium.[9] Indonesian states apparently needed to draw Lampung into their political sphere; a stone inscription at Palas Pasemah, for example, indicates that Srivijaya made a tactical thrust into south Lampung during its nascent years (late seventh century A.D.).[10]

In their heyday, Srivijaya and other Sumatran trading states generated wealth, confidence, and an international perspective. Southeast Sumatra was an important waystation on the journey from China to India and a center for Buddhist learning. Pilgrims from east Asia traveled with one monsoon to the Sumatran coast, and sojourned there to study religious texts and language while awaiting the seasonal change of winds that would carry them to the monasteries of northeast India. Most Srivijayan art was executed in ephemeral materials such as brick and wood; the few seventh- and eighth-century sculptures that survive resemble (and often surpass in quality) Javanese stone reliefs and bronzes of the same period. It is these early Javanese temple reliefs (and, by inference, their lost Sumatran counterparts) which, in their verisimilitude, offer the closest visual parallels to *tampan pasisir*. The formal, framed composition of a ship

30

with fluttering flags, birds in the sky, and fish-filled sea at central Java's late eighth-century Borobudur temple (fig. 12) may be compared to *tampan* No. 31; and the heaven-sent rain of blossoms in Buddhist reliefs and paintings resembles the drifting flowers of *tampan pasisir*.[11]

The cosmopolitan Srivijayan period (roughly, A.D. 650–1400) is the most probable era for the Indianized elaboration of imagery unique to *tampan pasisir*, which exudes an atmosphere of pride and self-assurance. However, the medium of choice—small, ritually powerful cloth squares fashioned in supplementary weft technique—may already have been established, as certainly was the ship motif. Textiles of *tampan*-like dimension, technique, and imagery (though more angular and stylized) were dispersed throughout Southeast Asia, and are still evident in isolated, widely separated areas: north Burma (fig. 13, page 80), upper Thailand, Laos, and south China.[12] All, these peoples are, or once were, Buddhists. Buddhism, which early evinced a proselytizing character, was the agent most capable of projecting iconography across such an extended region, and of permanently embedding images in many otherwise unrelated weaving vocabularies. Trees of life and vegetal motifs, apposed zoomorphs (especially peacocks and other birds, or quadrupeds such as lions), temple structures, umbrellas, elephants as vehicles of prestige, and elegant foliate meanders are all associated, collectively, with Buddhism. Shared usages of *tampan*-like cloths among these insular and mainland peoples may be based on early Buddhist customs, such as the offering of cloths at temples to earn merit and promote a higher rebirth[13] (see Nos. 33, 34). Etymological data also supports religious associations with *tampan*.[14] Srivijaya, though Buddhist, was probably too late and too localized in the western archipelago to reach and profoundly affect distant inland locales such as Yunnan. Unlike *tampan pasisir*, *tampan* from the interior of Lampung, and most mainland *tampan*-like textiles, exhibit very little of the Indian realism that traveled to Southeast Asia in the seventh to eleventh centuries. Rather, their symmetrical angularity and tendency to dense, hooked geometrics pertain to China and the Central Asian Steppes, and belong to an earlier era. The mingling in *tampan* and their mainland counterparts of Indian Buddhist usage and imagery, early Chinese and Steppic visual vocabulary, and tribal ritual concerns is difficult to account for during the Srivijayan period.

One feasible explanation may, however, be found in the early first millennium A.D. Buddhism made its initial Far Eastern appearance in Tonkin, north Vietnam, during India's Kushan dynastic era (first to third century A.D.). The Kushan were an east Scythian nomadic people, originally located on the Central Asian borders of China, who in the course of their progress southward from inner Asia toward eventual control of the Indian subcontinent absorbed artistic influences from west Asia and the Hellenized Mediterranean, adding finally rich Indian traditions to their own Steppic heritage. As rulers of India, the Kushan maintained trade contacts from Rome to China via Central Asia's Silk Road and the Malay Archipelago, in an ancient Asian world far more integrated than is commonly imagined. Vietnam was an important station on this trade and pilgrimage sea-lane; products of imperial Rome have been found in ancient Indochinese emporiums. Several of Southeast Asia's great river systems flow through or near Vietnam, affording access to interior weaving regions and providing also a "highway"—heavily traveled in both directions since prehistoric times—for direct Central Asian contact with Southeast Asia. As the first Southeast Asian state, Funan in South Vietnam, declined in the fourth to fifth century, new seafaring states in the Sunda Strait region near Lampung rose to prominence. Indonesia's most picturesque bronze kettledrums probably come from Tonkin (see text, No. 19). The close resemblance of drum iconography to that on Lampung *tapis* (women's skirts, Nos. 40–43) almost certainly dates or derives from art styles that spread during this period. The drums feature ships with animal bowsprits, houses with high gables, sacrificial scenes, men wearing plumed vegetal headdresses, horses and Steppic horsemen, creatures with many-tined antlers or huge horns, elongated *tumpal* borders, complex

Fig. 12. Stone relief, Borobudur, central Java, ca. 8th century

31

geometric designs (stars, rectilinear forms, and angular spirals), and the like. Inscriptions with specific Buddhist terminology have been found on a few kettledrums,[15] suggesting the possibility that at least some drums—the later, elaborate, pictorial types most pertinent to Lampung textile iconography—were brought to Indonesia and reached their present widespread distribution around the archipelago with Buddhist travelers or missions embarking from Indochina.

In short, Buddhist penetration of Indonesia from continental east Asia as well as directly from India is an intriguing hypothesis, because no other single locality or epoch supplies the intersection of influences that together establish the basic vocabulary of *tampan* and many other Lampung textiles; in fact, Indians, Indo-Scythians, and Chinese were gathered in Tonkin at that time.[16] Furthermore, the south China borderlands were almost certainly the original mainland home of Austronesians (the larger ethno-linguistic group to which Indonesians belong), and Austronesians may have maintained contact or residence there well into the historical period under discussion.

In later centuries, south Sumatran political and economic power waned under challenge by more stable Javanese competitors, and then collapsed with the arrival of Portuguese power in 1511. Lampung was somewhat shielded from, and even a beneficiary of, these events because its location allowed it to turn for patronage from Sumatra to Java (such was the case in Lampung's late relationship with Banten, a state erected just across the strait with crucial support from Sumatran and Chinese traders displaced by the Portuguese). During the late medieval Majapahit and Banten periods, from about 1300 to 1700, the tendency of Lampung art to extravagant detail intensified. As west Indonesian societies saw their real political and economic power diminished by increasing international competition for advantage in trade, they may have indulgently glorified their cultural traditions in *tampan* imagery. Indonesian literature of this late period contains pointed allusions to a cultural environment with features like those seen in *tampan pasisir* (for example, rulers with large retinues who sail from port to port, laden with prestige goods). However, the evolution of Lampung imagery probably ended no later than 1700; eighteenth-century *tampan* and other textile fragments show clearly that throughout the period of surviving Lampung textiles, there was a progressive decline in iconographic intelligibility, complexity, and artistry.

In sum, *tampan pasisir* seem to have grafted the sophisticated composition and realism of Indian classical art during Srivijayan times onto a preexisting Buddhist predilection for square, highly charged, sacred cloths. The great ships that reached out to the civilized world represented, in *tampan* imagery, an organizing principle that symbolized Lampung society; but beneath the cosmopolitan splendor lay the ancestral concerns of old tribal Indonesia, preserved both in *tampan* usage and in the local ethnic detail of *tampan* iconography.

1. For a more detailed discussion of *tampan pasisir*, see Holmgren and Spertus 1980; Holmgren et al. 1991.
2. Mirror symmetry, while easily accomplished on the loom, may originate in the concept of uniting upperworld- and underworld-ships on a single sacred axis; see Schärer 1942, fig. 6.
3. Schärer 1963, p. 137.
4. Ibid., plate xx, ill. 23.
5. See also Holmgren and Spertus 1980, fig. 6; Steinmann 1946, p. 1876.
6. Manguin 1986, p. 197.
7. Schärer 1963, pp. 204ff.
8. Wheatley 1983, p. 271.
9. This was the probable period of Indonesia's "colonization" of Madagascar. Bellwood (1985, p. 124) believes on linguistic grounds that the Indonesian migration postdates A.D. 400. However, it is possible that the Madagascar "outpost" is a remnant of wider Indonesian trade relationships in the western Indian Ocean, probably aimed ultimately at the Mediterranean world and belonging to an earlier date. See Holmgren et al. 1991.
10. The inscription of A.D. 682 is near Kalianda (Boechari 1979). Whether this represented for Srivijaya a brief sortie, a confrontation with a state located in Lampung, an effort to control the Sunda Strait, or a drive toward Java is unknown.
11. Delhi [1957], p. 41, plate ii.
12. Cheesman 1988, figs. on pp. 34, 88, 106.
13. Gittinger 1985. Forthcoming works that elucidate the relationships between *tampan*, Buddhism, and early Southeast Asian states are Gittinger 1989; Holmgren and Spertus 1989a; Holmgren et al. 1991.
14. In Java and Sumatra, the word *tampan* denotes a tray (usually wood or brass) for offerings (ceremonial presentations are a main usage of Lampung *tampan* textiles). In Malaya, an "oblong piece of ornamental cloth, usually yellow . . . worn (or rather carried) on the left shoulder when attending court" was called *tetampan* (or *tampan-tampan*), Wilkinson 1957, p. 1215; yellow has religious associations because saffron is the color of monks' robes. See also the *tampan*-like woman's shawl from Aceh, north Sumatra, in Yoshimoto 1977–78, vol. 2, plate 245. In religious epics written in Old Javanese (including the earliest, composed before A.D. 930), the verbs *anampa*[*ni*], *tinampa*[*n*] mean to carry or support on the palm of the hands (especially the paraphernalia carried in state in front of a person of high rank), to receive (on the hands), or to accept; *nanampan* means "salver." The Old Javanese root word is *tampa*. Zoetmulder 1982, pp. 1921–22.
15. Bernet Kempers 1988, pp. 283–84.
16. Wheatley 1983, pp. 263–73, 371ff.

32

33, 34. TWO *TAMPAN* (RITUAL WEAVINGS)

Kalianda district, southeast Lampung
19th century
Cotton; supplementary weft

33. 88 × 78 cm (34½ × 30½ in.) [↕]

34. 94 × 80 cm (37 × 31½ in.) [↕]
    Published: Holmgren and Spertus 1980,
    fig. 3.

Kalianda, a Lampung district at the southernmost tip of Sumatra, produced *tampan* in a distinct, local style. Most Kalianda *tampan* display a single stylized ship with many hooked oars dipping into the water beneath the hull, and high prows that curl inward (see *palepai* Nos. 36, 37). In contrast to the realism of *tampan pasisir* ships (Nos. 29–32), Kalianda *tampan* vessels are emblematic, their multiple tiers ordered by a commanding symmetrical plan. Human figures, sacred dwellings, trees of life, and prestige beasts crowd an atmosphere astir with tiny blue and red dots. The palette of Kalianda *tampan* is distinctively warm and sunny: deep red, pale and dark blue, ochre, and occasionally taupe, on a luminous cream-colored ground.

Kalianda overlooks the entrance of the Sunda Strait, immediately across from Java. Many Kalianda aristocrats assert that they are descended from Javanese. Lampung's last (sixteenth- and seventeenth-century) precolonial rulers governed from Banten in west Java, and Lampungers throughout the south coast adopted with pride many elements of Banten court culture. Although some claims to Banten–Javanese lineage may merely reflect past attempts to gain status and strengthen local legitimacy by association, Kalianda imagery often does relate more to Javanese than to *pasisir* conventions. The giants seen on Kalianda *tampan* No. 34, for example, resemble puppets of the Javanese *wayang* shadow theater, and the large solid tree forms that rise from the root-mound at top center parallel the trees or forested mountains (*kayon* and *gunungan*) located at center stage. The horror vacui and the runs of repeating color sequences in Kalianda textiles are reminiscent of *wayang beber*, Java's earliest extant paintings.[1]

Notwithstanding these similarities, any conclusion that Kalianda *tampan* (and *tampan pasisir* in general) are merely derivatives of Javanese art is undermined by examples from outside the archipelago that share *tampan* imagery. Cambodian silk ikats depict temples with fronds that hang from the gables, like those on the small shrines on deck in No. 33.[2] Shan (north Burmese) woven banners (fig. 13), suspended from tall poles erected near

a monastery, display temples with Kalianda-like tiered roofs,[3] "and generally a boat, in which a passenger is being rowed across a river by one or more boatmen, and the water is full of fish. . . . The poles and streamers are raised in memory of the dead." Baskets of grain are affixed to these poles; as people raise a "joyful shout, hundreds of birds . . . fly to the baskets to eat the grain"

Fig. 13. Memorial banner, Shan people, north Burma, ca. 1908. After Milne, *Shans at Home* (1910), fig. opposite p. 122

33

(*tampan* birds also throng near masts).[4] The fish, two boatmen, and masts surmounted with a pulley box shown in fig. 13 correspond closely to details in *tampan* No. 30; the symmetrical shape of the Shan ship and its boatmen resemble imagery in *lau pahudu* No. 8.

The occurrence of textiles sharing this specific format in dispersed areas of Southeast Asia places *tampan* in a larger context, and may illuminate their original use and meaning. Shan legend ascribes the origin of the banners that hang near temples to a poor widow who spent her last coins on materials to weave a narrow cloth as a gift for the Buddha. Although the cloth was disdained as useless by the Buddha's disciples, he declared her gift the greatest he had ever received because she had given him all that she possessed.[5] Gittinger has suggested that *tampan* are related to sitting mats carried by Buddhist monks;[6] revered Lampung mats called *lampit* resemble *tampan* in size and often in pattern.[7] In Lampung, as well as in Java and Palembang, a man's rank determined the number of cushions or mats on which he sat—probably an extension of the ancient concept that gods and their terrestrial representatives (kings) sit on cushions. Similarly, the use of multiple panels of *tampan* (or *palepai*, Nos. 36, 37) was often a prerogative of aristocrats (see also No. 35, which was allegedly made for a king).

Most likely, the iconographic vocabulary of Kalianda *tampan* was not derived from, but rather shared with, textiles from Java and other lands. In fact, there is no evidence that textiles like *tampan* or *palepai* (Nos. 36, 37) were ever produced on Java; however, it would be very surprising—considering the presence of *tampan*-like textiles on Bali and Lombok (No. 35)—if the Javanese also did not at some time weave similar textiles.

1. These features are particularly evident in the set of *wayang beber* scrolls at Wonosari, central Java. For two details, see Holmgren and Spertus 1989a.
2. Ibid.
3. Central pyramid-shaped structures, with multiple stacked gables (as in No. 33), were probably, in the original trade textiles, temples or sacred arches within which an enthroned Buddhist deity—or a tree, an earlier symbol of the Buddha—was depicted. In mainland Southeast Asia, a central Buddhist temple is commonly flanked by two small subsidiary temples.
4. Milne 1910, p. 123, and figs. opposite pp. 122, 124.
5. Ibid., p. 122.
6. Gittinger 1985.
7. Solyom 1984, fig. 12.

34

35. RITUAL CLOTH WITH NINE TABLEAUX
    (*SUBAHANILA?*)

Selaparang(?), central Lombok
19th century
Cotton; discontinuous supplementary weft
463 × 48 cm (182½ × 19 in.) [↕]

Two unusual textiles from Indonesian cultures other than Lampung are illustrated in this volume, the present weaving and *sungkit* No. 45, because they exemplify the wide dispersion of particular trade-textile forms, techniques, or imagery. This cloth, a spectacular survivor of the Sasak culture of Lombok, illustrates the continuity of ancient *pasisir* culture across the entire western archipelago. Palette, proportion, iconography, and technique are remarkably similar to those of coastal *tampan* (Nos. 29–34). The Sasak language, which is related to both Javanese and Balinese, and Sasak legends, which tell of ancient ties with Sumatran and Javanese kingdoms, both reflect broad cultural interconnections. In the eighteenth century, Balinese noblemen overthrew the Sasak kingdom based in Selaparang, where the present textile, allegedly made for the king, was obtained.

Balinese and Sasak both wove *tampan*-like textiles, called *osap* in Lombok. However, we know of only one other example that is figural rather than simply floral or geometric, a single-panel *osap* that displays four "horses"; it was found in northeast Lombok, the last remaining Sasak enclave on that island.[1]

Detail, No. 35

In the present piece, nine contiguous *tampan*-sized panels are woven with continuous warps. In Lampung also, thirteen hundred kilometers to the west, *tampan* were often made in multiples of two or more panels with continuous warps, then cut apart for individual use (a few *tampan* series that were never cut still survive[2]). Related examples in mainland Southeast Asia suggest that such series of squares were originally intended not to be cut, but folded to form a stack or hung from poles as festival banners (fig. 13, and text, Nos. 33, 34).

The presence of an unmistakeable trade-textile pattern on this cloth (third panel from the bottom) strengthens by association our contention that the animal, bird, and *wayang* figural imagery of the textile's other panels formerly appeared on trade textiles as well. This particular geometric pattern occurs in more or less elaborate form on the cloths of many Indonesian island cultures: Lampung red *tapis* ikat (No. 42) and supplementary weavings,[3] Borneo *sungkit* (No. 45), early Balinese *cepuk*,[4] and Toraja ikat, among others.[5] The wide geographical dispersion of this and other such core patterns corroborates the "prototype textile" hypothesis: that special cloths passed in trade throughout the archipelago during early periods from which textiles no longer survive, and reached all the cultures where local versions have been found.[6] This particular pattern appears on numerous early Indian trade cottons (chintz), primarily prints—popular trade items, but lacking the authority, technical difficulty, or exclusivity and luxuriousness that appealed to Indonesian aristocrats. Indeed, in 1978 a genuine Gujarati silk *patola* bearing this pattern surfaced (in Lampung), proving that a prestigious prototype did exist.[7] Historical evidence suggests that *patola* commanded the ranking position among prototype textiles after about the twelfth century; earlier prototypes included chintz, *tampan*-like textiles, and probably other unidentified genres as well.

1. Reproduced in Maxwell 1990, chapter 2 (Australian National Gallery, Canberra, acc. no. 1986.2454). For other examples in Bali and Lombok, see Khan Majlis 1984, pp. 70, 72, 78; Yoshimoto 1977–78, vol. 1, plate 18. Lampung examples, such as ibid., vol. 2, plate 194, are virtually indistinguishable from Lombok *osap*.
2. Khan Majlis 1984, fig. 151.
3. Langewis and Wagner 1964, plate 110.
4. Holmgren and Spertus 1989a.
5. Bühler and Fischer 1979, vol. 2, plates 72–73.
6. Holmgren 1983; Holmgren and Spertus 1989a; Holmgren et al. 1991.
7. Holmgren and Spertus 1989b.

36–39. FOUR LARGE CEREMONIAL HANGINGS

36. *Palepai*
Kesugian village, Kalianda district,
southeast Lampung
19th century
Cotton, silk, gold gimp; supplementary
weft, embroidery
246 × 54 cm (97 × 21½ in.) [↔]

37. *Palepai*
Kalianda district, southeast Lampung
19th century
Cotton, silk, gold gimp; supplementary weft
224 × 56 cm (88 × 22 in.) [↔]
Published: Holmgren and Spertus 1980,
fig. 26.

38. Beaded hanging
South central Lampung
Probably 18th century
Beads, rattan, cotton, and nassa shells
123 × 412 cm (48½ × 162 in.)

39. *Palepai* (?)
Lampung
Mid-19th century
Cotton, silk, mica flakes, gold gimp;
embroidery, appliqué
207 × 66 cm (81½ × 26 in.) [↔]

Kalianda *palepai* with single red ships flanked by two eccentric trees of life (Nos. 36, 37) make a unique and powerful statement. The ships, long and dignified, have sweeping oars and multiple prows that unfurl gracefully in a clear, luminous atmosphere. The trees are spiky and dynamic—one gnarled, one smooth. Aristocrats, together with prestige beasts, line the decks. As in Kalianda *tampan* (No. 33), pairs of smaller houses flank large central pavilions. The medallions displayed in the hull of No. 37 suggest anthropomorphs (more explicitly represented in No. 38, and in fig. 12, p.76).[1] Small lifeboats trail the great ships, schools of squid and fish dapple the water, and birds soar overhead.

Kalianda *palepai* usually display two ships,[2] more elongated than Kalianda *tampan* vessels, such as that in No. 33, but clearly derived from them. Multipaneled *tampan* that show repeating ships or houses (often erroneously called *palepai* by local people) may represent an intermediate step in the conceptualization of the double-ship *palepai*[3] (the name *palepai* is probably cognate with the Old Javanese word *lepih*, meaning "to fold, double, duplicate"; compare also No. 35). Single-ship *palepai* represent a further intellectual and formal devel-

opment of the *tampan* format: an encompassing unity, symbolizing the consolidation of two lineages (represented in No. 37 as different trees with figures standing in the branches), expressed in the breadth and extension of the one ship.

Aristocrats, the mainstays of the "ship of state," were the exclusive owners of *palepai*, which hung behind them at formal meetings, marriages, ceremonies that established new social units, and eventually in death. In Kalianda, the iconographic content of *palepai* sometimes reflected the ceremonial context in which they were displayed. Thus, in the final phases of marriage rites, a single-ship *palepai* replaced a double ship, to signify the merger of family clans or the joining of male and female. When *palepai* ceased to be woven in Kalianda, plaited rattan versions were made,[4] as well as abstract patchwork cloths of *palepai* size.

Palepai are found only in south Lampung near the coast. In 1883, the paroxysmal eruption of Krakatau in the Sunda Strait generated forty-meter waves that swept away nearly all the seaside villages of south Lampung; over thirty-five thousand people died, and Kalianda town—in direct sight of the cone—literally disappeared. During World War II, many traditional textiles were cut apart to make clothing (Japanese occupation forces diverted factory-made textiles to their armies). The few remaining *palepai* were generally valued more as inheritance goods, to be equitably apportioned among descendants, than as objects of inherent beauty. *Palepai* No. 36 was divided in half before 1970 for two brothers; one half was later subdivided again into four. Two additional strips (never recovered) were cut off for use as patches and rags. Fortunately, a field photograph from the 1960s facilitated the reassembly of the various fragments, and the reconstruction of lost parts.[5]

Beaded hanging No. 38, although displayed on a wall like *palepai*, has the grand scale and stunning visual impact of an entire temple façade. Only three small, *tampan*-sized bead pieces, each displaying ships, were collected by Dutch institutions before World War II;[6] a few additional beadwork examples on rattan foundations are now documented.[7]

Here, two great boats counterpoise beside a monumental mountain or tree (also ship borne). In the background, a starry night seems to modulate from left to right into day. Flame or growth bursts from every image. Large, swelling forms further emphasize the impression of grandeur. As in Kalianda *tampan*, the central pyramid generally resembles *gunungan* or *kayon*, mountain- or tree-shaped forms that provide the focal point on the Javanese *wayang* theater stage and separate opposing or complementary groups of characters. The holy mountain—or tree of life—where divinity dwells may represent the underlying unity of an essentially dualistic philosophy of life which requires that good meet evil, that sky touch earth, that night alternate with day. The entire triangular form is composed of patches of color. In early Indian and Central Asian painting of the fifth century and later, mountains are frequently stylized as piled blocks of color.[8] Patchwork has for millennia carried evocative religious associations: the Buddha wore patchwork in humility; priests, saints, and kings wear it in association with the godhead.[9] Patchwork protects, and symbolizes piety.[10]

The large ship at left holds a shrine or sacred house with closed double doors, like that depicted in the *kayon* of the Javanese puppet theater.[11] A small figure peers from the gable, echoing the larger figure standing on the rooftop, whose stylized head looks like that of the embroidered figures on *tapis* No. 40. The ship at right, in rising light, may carry a throne (Lampung *pepadon*, seats of merit, often have finials like those described by the white-on-black pattern seen here).

The large old ceramic and glass beads on this hanging—both European and Asian in origin, and weighing altogether some seventy kilograms—are more sonorous than the tidy trade beads that decorate Sumba or Toraja pieces. Costly and precious, beads were sparingly applied in Lampung, primarily to belts and small rattan boxes. This hanging, analogous in its lavishness to a treasure encrusted with jewels, must have belonged to a king or high-ranking aristocrat.

The strings of beads are disposed in painterly fashion, densely packing areas with color and, like brushstrokes, freely shifting linear direction. Arranged in curves, they create a flowing effect like the silk-embroidered background of *tapis* (see, for example, No. 40), which they closely resemble in rhythm and line. Beads of differing hues mingle pointillistically, yielding rich textured tones.

This hanging was undoubtedly displayed on a wall. Colonial-period records name one small beaded mat *tampan maju*, and another *kain pelamar ratu*. These terms indicate that beaded *tampan* represented dowry wealth: *maju* means "bride," *pelamar ratu* means "ask for a 'royal' hand in marriage" (brides are equated with queens). A local informant reported that another large beaded mat was used for meditation, which associates these pieces with the sphere of religion.

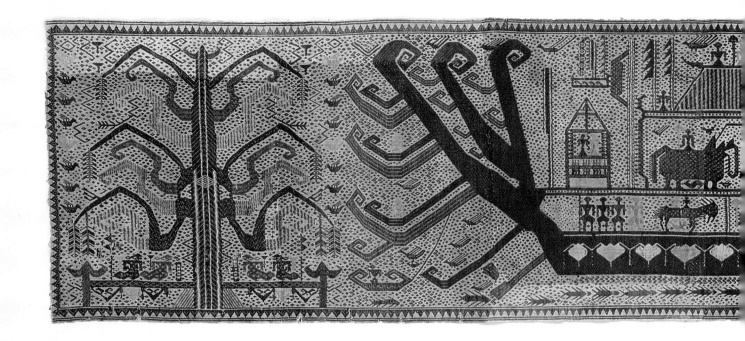

Top: No. 36
Bottom: No. 37

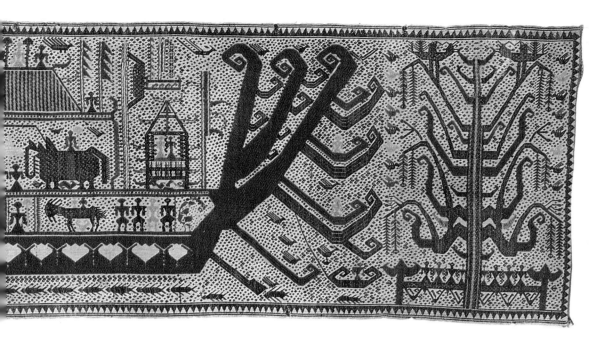

38

No. 39 is the only embroidered *palepai* known to us. In composition it relates directly to the great beaded hanging No. 38—two ships on either side of a towering pyramidal mountain form—but its atmosphere is altogether different. Whereas the impact of No. 38 is one of immensity, unremitting and regal, No. 39 is intimate and unpretentious. Delicately described with curvilinear golden needlework, its images glow against an open ground of midnight blue. Tiny mica mirrors, scattered like dewdrops, sparkle with reflected light. Serpentine floral motifs, voluptuously oversized, seem to engulf the ships on every side. The sun beams at one side, the moon on the other (in the creation myth of Borneo's Ngaju people, the sun and moon marry[12]). Embroidered lines are crisp and inventive; lush foliate meanders metamorphose as they unfurl.

Freed from the linear pattern constraints of warp and weft inherent in weaving, this *palepai* approaches, more nearly than any preceding piece, the freehand quality of drawing and painting. Although its iconogra-

phy derives mainly from the traditional Lampung textile vocabulary—birds, fish, small shrines, curling "inner hulls," large rudders, stylized figures, and so forth—its elaborately decorative style shows strong affinities with art of the Islamic period (after 1500) from Java, Bali, Lombok, and Borneo. Flags that display a sword with two blades surmount each *palepai* ship. Similar swords are the prominent central motif on triumphal old Islamic batik banners probably made in Cirebon, a west-central Java *pasisir* port with deeply spiritual Islamic art traditions.[13]

An unconventional Javanese wall hanging dating to about 1830 in the Rijksmuseum voor Volkenkunde, Leiden, presents an interesting parallel to this hanging.[14] Painted on paper that was applied to a cotton backing decorated with gold foil and embroidery, the painting illustrates the wanderings and quests of the legendary Jaka Prataka, who eventually became the king of Egypt. The tale belongs to a tradition of picaresque Islamic romances, "stories about warlike adventures and fabulous travels, of the kind of tales of Sindbad the Sailor . . . [which] suited the taste of the rising mercantile and ruling classes of sixteenth and seventeenth century Pasisir towns."[15] Like No. 39, the Leiden wall hanging displays a ship with a scalloped hull, curly vegetal growth at the prows that resembles seaweed, sea creatures beneath the ship, a second tier of "decks," and florid ornamentation. The sentiments of such popular tales, and their illustrations (probably common in the medieval *pasisir* world), may have spurred the mannered, courtly elaboration of some Lampung art styles—the multiple-deck arrangement in *tampan* No. 32, for example, or the pairs of conversing courtiers in architectural compartments.

The most compelling parallels with *palepai* No. 39, however, appear in carved or painted objects made by the animist Ngaju peoples of Borneo.[16] These artifacts suggest that the late Islamic attributes of No. 39 are superficial accretions to a much older tradition. Schärer convincingly relates "soul ships" made by the Ngaju in south Borneo to funeral customs and beliefs about the

39

dead,[17] and also to the arrival of ancestors (the "Sun People") from the upperworld; for the Ngaju, the coming to earth, and eventual return of forebears to the ancestral realm (after they have been transformed into hawks or water snakes), constitutes a profound unity. In Ngaju culture, and perhaps in Lampung as well, the boats themselves represent the "total godhead."[18]

1. Oarsmen peer out from "portholes" in some *tampan* hulls, e.g., Holmgren and Spertus 1980, fig. 25. See also fig. 12, page 76.
2. See, for example, Gittinger 1979, fig. 48.
3. Ibid., fig. 51.
4. Solyom 1984, fig. 13.
5. Gittinger 1972, plate 87.
6. For the examples at the Museum Nasional, Jakarta: Tillmann 1938a, p. 12 (acc. no. 577), and [Jakarta] 1940, opposite p. 168 (acc. no. 23299). For the piece at the Tropenmuseum, Amsterdam: Van Brakel et al. 1987, color plate 28.
7. Gittinger 1979, no. 60; Maxwell 1990, chapter 3 (Australian National Gallery, Canberra, acc. no. 1983.3689); Solyom 1984, fig. 24; and Maxwell 1990, chapter 5 (Australian National Gallery, Canberra, acc. no. 1983.3690).

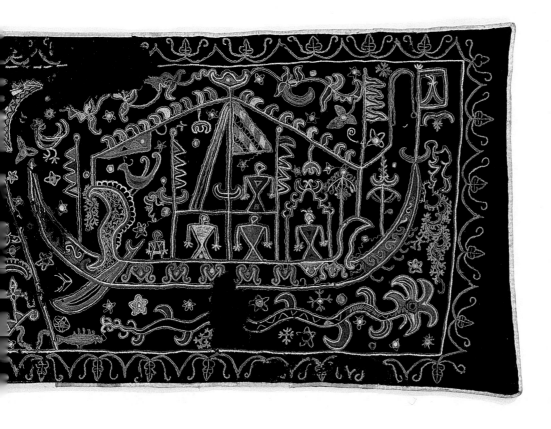

Numerous small areas of hanging No. 38 have been restored. Its original condition illustrates why so few beaded objects survive. Disintegrating, damaged by insects and vermin, and with sections missing along the perimeters where it had been nailed to walls, the piece was being scavenged for its beads; only one short section of nassa-shell border remains, lower left.

8. Pal 1975, plate 57.
9. Ibid., plate 5; Veldhuisen-Djajasoebrata 1984, plates on pp. 77, 78.
10. See Hardjonagoro 1980, p. 227.
11. Rassers 1959, plate I.
12. Schärer 1963, p. 181.
13. See, for example, Kartiwa et al. 1976, no. 14, a large, late nineteenth-century flag that was acquired from central Javanese rulers, and which is inscribed in Arabic with affirmations of faith. See also Feldbauer 1988, p. 117.
14. Galis et al. 1970, no. 296 (pp. 142ff.).
15. Pigeaud 1967, p. 220.
16. Steinmann 1946, third example in fig. 19, is representative.
17. Schärer 1963, pp. 91ff., figs. 8–10.
18. Ibid., p. 137; "soul ships" appear in ills. 8, 11, 22, and 23.

40–43. FOUR *TAPIS* (WOMEN'S CEREMONIAL SKIRTS)

Lampung, south Sumatra
19th century
Silk, cotton; embroidery, warp ikat
Formerly, tubular garments seamed at warp
ends (now open)[1]

40. 133 × 131 cm (52½ × 51½ in.) [↕]

41. 136 × 118 cm (53½ × 46½ in.) [↕]

42. 131 × 114 cm (51½ × 45 in.) [↕]

43. 134 × 119 cm (53 × 47 in.) [↔]

Fluid line, varied pattern, and a confident integration of energized detail, suffused throughout with an odor of fertility and frank eroticism, make *tapis* a high-water mark in Indonesian weaving—although their complex iconographic intent remains almost entirely conjectural.

The haunting primordial forms of No. 40 characterize one of the best-known *tapis* genres. Comparison among many related examples suggests that these large

Fig. 14. Bronze vessel found at Kerinci, northwest Sumatra. After Bernet Kempers, *The Kettledrums of Southeast Asia* (1988), fig. 22.11a

Detail, No. 40

undulating figures—suspended, like amoebas under a microscope, in a primeval watery realm—represent anthropomorphs, or spirits with seemingly human features.[2] Frequently they bear young within them, as if impregnated with future generations (see detail). Bursts of foliage shoot from their bodies, spring from the coil of their tails, or hang latent in long-stemmed buds. Bodily limbs often melt into foliage. The entire vision evokes generation—an impression sustained by *tapis* Nos. 41, 42, and 43. Themes of fertility and genealogy occur also in Sumba and Toraja textiles (Nos. 1–3, 25), though visualized in very different form.

The embroidered lines are supple and alive. Rippling waves caress the main figures and activate the ground. Strands of silk are not twisted into thread but worked raw, as flat bundles, to yield shimmering planes of color uninterrupted by individual stitches. The juxtaposition of smooth unfurling shapes against a textured ground strikingly resembles a similar stylistic convention on ancient Bronze Age vessels found in west Indonesia (fig. 14).

40

Detail, No. 41

Nos. 41, 42, and 43 represent a fascinating, newly documented *tapis* group.[3] The genre is characterized by a single central embroidered band (typically, *tapis* have two bands) and ikat panels with great ships or rich burgundy abstractions. Narrow embroidered meanders decorate the hem and waist. The embroidered iconography includes large, lavishly detailed anthropomorphs (No. 41) and strangely interlocked forms (No. 42), quite different from the usual *tapis* repertoire of boats, trees, and diminutive stick figures.

Tapis needlework is a visual tour de force. In No. 41, each of the anthropomorphs wears a swirling headdress strewn with flowers and jewels that brushes the swelling sexual parts of the figure above (compare Nos. 2, 3). Each figure is subtly individuated. Hyphenated red-and-white lines that spiral beside the ears terminate in petite, dark-colored blossoms; tiny single-thread spirals tickle a figure's genitals, which burst into bloom; deep-hued threads highlight minuscule ever-varying details, inviting the eye to explore beyond the initial dazzle of the primary white forms; often the thrust of a full curve carries through to resolve in a single thread. This central embroidered band may depict an ancestral lineage, a stream of generation.

The ikat panels of No. 41 (rotated ninety degrees from the visual orientation of its embroidery) present dramatic dyed tableaux unknown in scholarly literature or early collections.[4] Ordinarily, *tapis* ikat (such as No. 40) displays iconography which, though intentional and detailed, is often indecipherable. In sharp contrast, the dramatically enlarged images of No. 41 are unambiguous: huge ships with trees of life on their prows hold a shrine;[5] an orant figure stands within, growth sprouting from its head (like the figures on the embroidered panel). The symmetry and formality of this ikat image parallel those of Kalianda *tampan* No. 33.

Deep burgundy-red ikat patterns of abstract design occur more frequently than large boats within this *tapis* genre. They imitate precious Indian *patola* patterns and thus provide a prestigious surround for the central embroidered statement. Examples of Indian *patola* that display some of these patterns still survive; other *tapis* patterns are so closely akin to characteristic *patola* palette and symmetries that almost certainly they were inspired by *patola* types no longer extant. This conclusion is supported by the appearance at localities far distant from each other of identical designs surely drawn from the same now-vanished trade-textile source. Ikat sections of No. 42, for example, preserve the same *patola* design as

41

Lombok ritual cloth No. 35, Borneo *sungkit* No. 45, and an original Gujarati silk *patola* discovered in Lampung (see text, No. 35).[6] In this respect, red *tapis* possess singular art-historical importance because they preserve prized ikat patterns, some unknown in any other form (such as No. 43), and thus constitute a veritable catalogue of early, lost trade designs.

The rich centerband embroidery of No. 42 probably shares the generational theme of No. 41: paired figures appear to be copulating (other related red *tapis* display clearly interlocked hindquarters). Undulating intermediate passages, perhaps arenas of conception, contain pairs of nascent outstretched "arms"; large central arrows thrust into the main figures (similar passages appear in No. 43).

No. 43, with two embroidered bands rather than one, is atypical of the red *tapis* group. Its ikat, though rich, does not have the bilaterally symmetrical appearance typical in *patola*, but rather evokes masklike motifs with tall verdant headdresses like those on Borneo ikat *pua* (large ritual textiles). The embroidered passage at far left in the detail resembles a Buddhist *vajra* ("thunderbolt" of inspiration and intellect). The mysterious white shapes at right in the detail suggest two recumbent anthropomorphs, their bushy genitalia reminiscent of Hindu *linga* (phallic sculptures that symbolize the generative essence of Siva the Creator) strewn with flowers, or the excited sexuality of the figures in No. 41. Tiny fan-shaped motifs with single-stitched lines recur throughout, like fragile stamen. Small boats carry fantastic figures with elaborate coiffures, and trees of life.

Influences from many different cultures and periods coalesce in *tapis*. The embroidered panels in particular owe a clear spiritual debt to art styles that developed in China and its southern borderlands during the approximate period 700 B.C. to A.D. 300. Close visual parallels to *tapis* iconography are expressed in mainland bronze, jade, lacquer, and other artifacts from this period, some of which found their way into the archipelago. The ancient bronze vessel excavated in Kerinci, northwest Sumatra (fig. 14, page 94), for example, was probably cast in the vicinity of Tonkin, north Vietnam. Tonkin was a site of early Buddhist establishments that may have been instrumental in the spread of Bronze Age culture in Indonesia, in the sowing of Buddhistic *tampan*-type customs among many Southeast Asian peoples, or even in the founding of early Indianized states in the archipelago (see text, Nos. 29–32). Quite apart from religion, the Vietnam region was a melting pot and

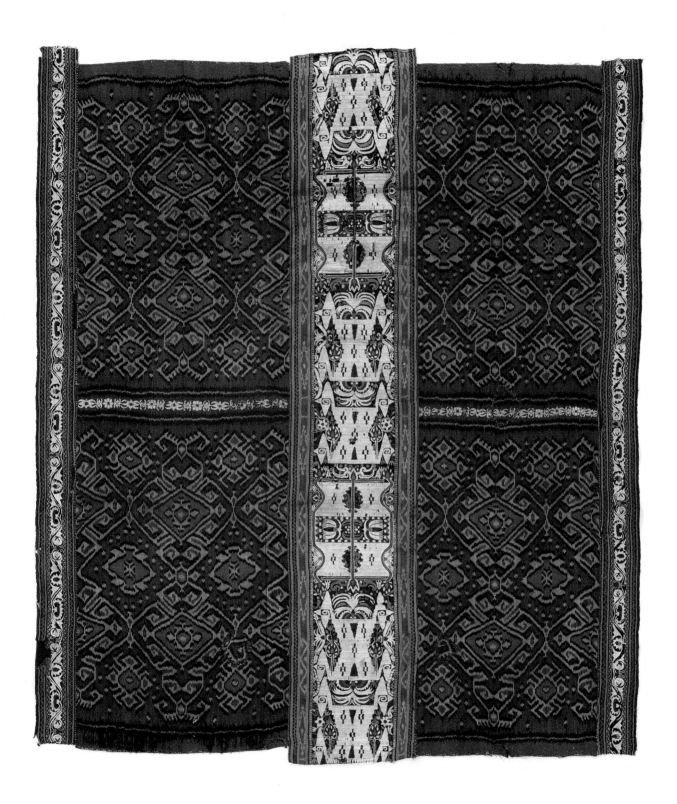

42

cradle of early Southeast Asian civilization, which welded Chinese, Indian, Central Asian, and dominant local elements into a powerful fusion culture, usually called "Dongson," after an important Tonkinese archaeological site. There is every reason to suppose that mainland textiles (for example, from China) also circulated in the archipelago, for during this period Indonesian peoples were pressing expansively in many different directions—into the Pacific, up to the African coast, and onto the Indochinese mainland itself—motivated at least in part by trade. Silk embroidery may have appeared first, in Lampung, on imported East or Southeast Asian textiles that looked very much like *tapis* (see also No. 44). Mainland bronzes and jades of the period offer depictions of lithe little people with fanciful headgear, soaring birds, fantastic animals, ships, geometric designs with rounded corners and sweeping *S* curves or spirals—often indistinguishable from those which appear on *tapis* made in the nineteenth century. This extraordinary visual continuity, extending over two millennia, is not unique to Lampung; Iban textiles from Borneo (and to a lesser extent Toraja weavings; see text, No. 19) exemplify the same phenomenon.

Ikat iconography often seems to issue from sources altogether different from those of embroidery; in many *tapis*, there is little visual or thematic relationship between these two technically and physically separate components of the one cloth. Some ikat panels, such as those seen in No. 40, display rectangular vignettes closely allied with early Dongsonian style. A few examples clearly indicate that originally schematic squatting human figures, long-necked birds, and houses-*cum*-ships bearing trees were intended; but most surviving examples are so highly abstracted that apparently the original signification gradually slipped from the weavers' grasp, until at last they simply copied by rote. In the *tapis* genre represented by No. 42, however, ikat patterns almost always derive from Indian textile models.

1. In this volume, *tapis* illustrations are aligned to accord with the visual orientation of *embroidered* iconography; when *tapis* were worn as skirts, however, the warp direction of the fabric was always horizontal [↔].
2. See, for example, Tillmann 1938b, fig. 15.
3. Two examples only appear in the standard literature: Langewis and Wagner 1964, plate 173 (Museum für Völkerkunde, Basel, acc. no. IIc 15952), and plate 179 (Tropenmuseum, Amsterdam, acc. no. 1319/4).
4. Less than ten *tapis* with huge ikat boat panels are known. All emerged concurrently (probably from one narrow locality or even one family collection) and are now dispersed mainly among Japanese and North American collections, e.g., the Detroit Institute of Arts, acc. no. 81.717.
5. The ship's hull here has slipped below the visual plane, but is clearly defined in the Detroit Institute of Arts example, note 4 above.
6. Holmgren and Spertus 1989b.

Detail, No. 43

43

44. SHOULDER CLOTH

Sabu, Lampung Bay
19th century
Cotton and silk; embroidery
224 × 34 cm (88 × 13½ in.) [↕].

Lampung's inventory of old textile genres includes many one-of-a-kind pieces, which hints at a repertoire formerly much wider than the surviving corpus. This slender shawl stands alone. Lustrous silk embroidery radiates against an empty, light-swallowing ground of midnight blue. The opposed triangular *tumpals* are packed with brilliant florals, and inhabited by what appear to be crustaceans (perhaps conceived as shrimp), described with broad maroon-and-brown strokes, whose "claws" in turn envelop a motif associated in *tapis* Nos. 41–43 with genitalia. Successive masklike motifs with mysterious outreaching "arms" appear in the textile's central rectangle and stare out from narrow inner bands separating the *tumpals*—perhaps, again, allusions to sex and generation. They bear a remarkably close resemblance to the thorny Toraja earrings called *tai janja* (or *tai ganja*, fig. 15), which are uninhibited variants in the large family of similarly shaped earrings that apparently represent female pudenda (the form occurs from Sumatra to the Philippines, and includes Sumba *mamuli* Nos. 4–6).[1]

Similar elaborately patterned, floriated *tumpals* appear on silk embroidered textiles from Palembang, where they were manufactured in a specialized cottage industry by Chinese-Indonesians. Although Palembang versions are seldom as intricate, suggestive, or artful as this

Detail, No. 44

Fig. 15. Toraja *tai janja* (pendant). Cast brass. Collection Anita E. Spertus and Robert J. Holmgren

example, the relationship is still close; quite possibly, Lampung weavers received the tradition of silk embroidery from the Chinese (who are mixed by marriage with the ethnic Lampung population to a greater degree than usual in Indonesia). The odd stylistic dissimilarity between ikat and embroidered panels of most *tapis*, and the fact that these panels are usually woven and finished separately and then sewn together, raises the possibility that embroidering was once a profession in Lampung that was pursued by specialist artisans.

The embroidery of this shoulder cloth is equally fine on both the obverse and reverse. Subtly finished warp fringe rolled into minute balls is characteristic also of early Sasak textiles called *sokong* from Lombok, and in all probability preserves an archaic and once widespread *pasisir* mark of quality.

1. Acquired by Toraja from Bugis traders, *tai janja* were treated (like *mamuli*) as bridewealth, and also strung on waistbands worn by children (Kruyt 1938, vol. 2, pp. 287–88). Kaudern illustrates two "ear pendants" attributed to north Celebes ("from China," according to his local informant) and to Batak peoples of north Sumatra, which are both indistinguishable from Toraja *tai janja* (Kaudern 1944, pp. 318–19; figs. 212-A, 214-A). If the arresting Batak attribution is accurate, then Kaudern's examples imply that earrings very close in shape to the present shawl motif must once have been an article of Southeast Asian trade. Indeed, in the west Chinese borderlands, shapes close to this shawl pattern—and many other *tapis* patterns besides—are common; they demonstrate that some Southeast Asian art styles bear clear signs of Steppic art: see, for example, Kazak Folk Art Designs Editorial Board 1980, plate 91, in which complex leafy *tumpals* contain the same "shrimp" and vaginal motifs as this shawl.

45. *PUA SUNGKIT* (CEREMONIAL CLOTH)

Iban peoples, Sarawak, east Malaysia
Mid-19th century
Cotton; discontinuous supplementary wrapping wefts
189 × 100 cm (74½ × 39½ in.) [↕]

Pua sungkit are the most precious textiles of the Iban ("Sea Dyak") tribes in northwest Borneo. Although late nineteenth-century English and Dutch collections contain a comprehensive array of Borneo ikat weavings, loincloths, jackets, beadwork, headgear, shawls, and mats, together with extensive notes about technique and use,[1] *pua sungkit* were completely overlooked. The numerous examples that gradually emerged from the field during the period 1975–85 defined a stunning and unexpected new level of quality because, as a class, *sungkit* are the earliest textiles of the Iban, and among the oldest and most interesting cloths to be found in greater Indonesia.

Many *sungkit* features are associated with the old trade-textile complex. The formal, *patola*-like organization of *pua sungkit* differs entirely from that of most ikatted Iban *pua*. The latter display weblike centerfield designs that interweave and interpenetrate in continuous ebb and flow,[2] whereas *sungkit* often consist of autonomous motifs repeated serially within a frame (for example, the rows of *antu*, "spirits," in the present example; compare Sumba *hinggi* No. 17). The lower portion of this textile displays an elegant version of a pattern seen also in Nos. 35 and 42; all are derived from Indian *patola*. Large rosettes top and bottom correspond in shape and placement to *patola* prototypes. Colors, too, conform to *patola*: natural undyed cotton and blue-black threads on a deep maroon ground (in a few rare examples of both *sungkit* and *patola*, the ground is yellow or dark indigo blue).

Iban textiles are considerably more sophisticated than those of other, neighboring Borneo tribes, possibly indicating a different historical experience. At least some exposure to outside cultures espousing art traditions more recent than the Dongsonian fusion style, which provides a foundation for Iban art, is certain. Some Iban assert that they (or, what is more likely, part of their elite) came centuries ago to west Borneo from Minangkabau, west-central Sumatra. Some contact with pre-Islamic central Sumatra is plausible; textile border patterns, badges, tapestry weaves, and gold-thread brocades are often very similar to those of the Batak and Minangkabau peoples. Although these affinities might also be attributed to admiration for the same trade textiles, many historical sources indicate that in the fourteenth and fifteenth centuries, movements of peoples from Sumatra toward northerly lands intensified. Interestingly, some clans from north Lampung (for example, Kenali) claim to have come originally from Minangkabau as well. These possible connections should be treated with caution; but the crucial light that Borneo casts on Lampung iconography brings to mind William Howell's early (1898) supposition that Sumatrans and other Islamicized Malays "were once what the Dyaks are now, in matters of civilization and religion."[3]

Specific information about *sungkit*, based on recently collected field data, is scant. *Sungkit* apparently played a central part in headhunting rites, which the Dutch and English suppressed at the turn of the twentieth century.[4] Contemporaneous English writers were clearly taken aback by the deep-rooted Dyak requirement for decapitated heads in many ceremonial contexts, by the Dyaks' eager anticipation of war, esteem for successful hunters, and "macabre" veneration of the spirits that inhabited the skulls. This reaction may explain why Europeans disregarded (or Iban declined to show) *sungkit*, which were used "nearly exclusively" to cradle head trophies, or "hung much as an altar cloth before which were placed offerings and human heads."[5] *Sungkit* also served to canopy shamans as they divined omens by inspecting pig liver.[6]

Sungkit are constructed in a difficult discontinuous supplementary weft-wrapping technique executed on the loom but with the use of a needle. Supplementary yarns encircle two or more warp threads between single strokes of weft. The resulting texture imparts a subtle velvety appearance. Produced with unconventional methods, *sungkit* were clearly very special textiles, apparently concealed from outsiders.

1. Important Iban collections are at the Museum of Mankind, London; the University Museum of Archaeology and Anthropology, Cambridge; and the Sarawak Museum, Kuching. The main colonial-period reference work is Haddon and Start 1936.
2. For example, Gittinger 1979, figs. 168, 171–73.
3. Howell 1963, p. 2.
4. A *sungkit* jacket (*kalambi*) at the University Museum of Archaeology and Anthropology, Cambridge, acc. no. 35.904, collected by Charles Hose about 1900, contains many rows of differently described "human" figures, the reported names of which, such as "brave man with war cap," "seem to indicate that [the jacket] was associated in some way with head-hunting" (Haddon and Start 1936, p. 46) or, at any rate, with religious ceremonies.
5. Watters n.d., p. [1].
6. Ibid.

GLOSSARY

batik Patterning technique. Coloring is controlled by application of wax or paste resist to some design areas of a fabric so that dye only penetrates uncoated areas.

cepuk Weft ikat wrap of cotton or silk. [Bali]

Dongson Vigorous Bronze Age art style influential throughout Southeast Asia during the period ca. 400 B.C.–A.D. 300 but derived from many Asian cultural forebears (tribal, Chinese) going back to the second millennium B.C. Dongson is best represented by iconography that appears on bronze artifacts, e.g. kettledrums. The core area for production of this material was probably north Vietnam (a representative sample was excavated in Dongson village).

geringsing Cotton double-ikat wrap, sarong, or ritual cloth. [Bali]

gunungan Pyramidal "mountain" form, a center-stage fixture of *wayang* theater with both temporal and spatial functions, used, for example, to punctuate episodes in performances and to physically separate antagonistic or complementary groups of characters; harmonizes opposing forces, and represents the eternal and the divine. Usually displays a gateway (to a temple) flanked by giants; a tree crowded with animals rises from its roof. Also called *kayon*. [Java and *pasisir* cultural areas]

hinggi Man's cotton ikat mantle or hip cloth; used also as a shroud. [Sumba]

ikat "To bind"; tie-dye patterning technique. Coloring is controlled by tightly binding portions of unwoven yarn with fiber to resist the penetration of dye, while unbound portions accept the color. The resulting patterned yarn, after being carefully aligned on the loom, is woven into cloth. The technique is usually executed on either the warp or the weft yarns, although fine double-ikats were made in India (*patola*) and Bali (*geringsing*).

kaki "Feet"; striped outer panels of an ikat shroud. [Toraja]

kayon "Tree-of-life"; see *gunungan*.

lau Woman's skirt. [Sumba]

lau hada Woman's ceremonial skirt decorated with shells. [Sumba]

lau katipa Woman's ceremonial skirt decorated with beads. [Sumba]

lau pahudu Woman's skirt decorated with supplementary warp technique. [Sumba]

mamuli Traditional omega-shaped ear ornament or pendant (*mamuli* is the Sumba term, but the essential form appears throughout the archipelago).

mawa', maa' Painted, printed, or resist-dyed ritual cloth. [Toraja]

mbesa tali to batu "Headcloth of the stone man"; see *pewo*. [Toraja]

osap Small *tampan*-like cotton supplementary weft textile. [Lombok]

pahudu Pattern guide for supplementary technique weaving; fashioned from split bamboo sticks and plied cotton. [Sumba]

palepai Large ceremonial hanging decorated with supplementary weft technique. [Lampung]

paporitonoling Cotton warp ikat ceremonial weaving. [Toraja]

pasisir "Coastal"; used also in this volume to denote the more sophisticated and cosmopolitan shared culture of coastal peoples, mainly in west Indonesia.

patola Long silk double-ikat from Gujarat, India; prized luxury trade items.

pelangi "Rainbow"; tie-dye patterning technique. Portions of woven fabric are gathered and tightly bound, either with fiber or, to describe delicate designs, by means of a needle (needle *pelangi* is called *tritik*). Immersed in dye, the fabric in the immediate area of the binding resists color, while the loosely gathered portions accept it.

pewo Headwrap or loincloth, woven with myriad selvedged slits and then tie-dyed; also called *mbesa tali to batu*. [Toraja]

porilonjong Large cotton ikat ceremonial hanging. [Toraja]

poritutu, porisitutu' Ikat ceremonial hanging or sarong. [Toraja]

pua Large ikat ceremonial cloth. [Iban]

pua sungkit Large *sungkit* ceremonial cloth. [Iban]

roto Long tie-dyed (*pelangi*) cotton festival banner. [Toraja]

sanggaran Branched wooden structure that marked places of offerings and sacrifice. [Borneo]

sarita Long narrow banner or wrap; painted, printed, or resist-dyed. [Toraja]

sarong Tubular skirt.

sekomandi Cotton ikat shroud. [Galumpang Toraja]

sekong Motif with four flexed arms, perhaps originally understood as anthropomorphic. [Toraja]

Srivijaya Thalassocratic state, ca. A.D. 650 – 1392, based probably in the vicinity of Palembang (southeast Sumatra), one of the most important and powerful Indonesian trading states.

sungkit Warp wrapping patterning technique. [Iban, Borneo]

tai janja Brass ornament strung from a waistband and used in gift exchange. [north Toraja]

tampan Small square ritual weaving patterned with supplementary weft technique. [Lampung]

tampan maju One name for a small beaded mat. [Lampung]

tampan pasisir *Tampan*, generally monochromatic, of a courtly, often pictorial style. [south coast of Lampung]

tapis Woman's ceremonial skirt. [Lampung]

tumpal Row of repeating triangles; one of Southeast Asia's most ancient motifs.

wayang "Shadow"; traditional epic theater usually performed by shadow puppets (*wayang kulit*) or actors (*wayang wong*). [Java and *pasisir* cultural areas]

wayang beber Painted scrolls that relate legendary narratives, unrolled during theatrical performance. [Java]

WORKS CITED

Adams, Monni
1966 "Tissus décorés de l'île de Sumba." *Objets et Mondes 6*, no. 1 (Spring), pp. 3–18. Paris: Musée de l'Homme.

1969 *System and Meaning in East Sumba Textile Design: A Study in Traditional Indonesian Art.* Southeast Asian Studies Cultural Report Series, no. 16. New Haven: Yale University.

1971 "Designs in Sumba Textiles: Local Meanings and Foreign Influences." *Textile Museum Journal* (Washington, D.C.) 3, no. 2 (December), pp. 28–37.

1974 "Symbols of the Organized Community in East Sumba, Indonesia." *Bijdragen tot de Taal-, Land- en Volkenkunde* 130, no. 2/3, pp. 324–47. Leiden: Koninklijk Instituut voor Taal-, Land- en Volkenkunde.

Adams, Monni, and Alit Djajasoebrata
1965 *Leven en dood op Sumba; Life and Death on Sumba.* Rotterdam: Museum voor Land- en Volkenkunde. Exhibition catalogue.

Adriani, N., and Albert C. Kruyt
1950–51 *De Bare'e sprekende Toradjas van Midden-Celebes.* 2nd rev. ed. 4 vols. Verhandelingen der Koninklijke Nederlandse Akademie van Wetenschappen (Afdeling Letterkunde), new series 54–56. Amsterdam.

Bellwood, Peter
1979 *Man's Conquest of the Pacific: The Prehistory of Southeast Asia and Oceania.* New York: Oxford University Press.

1985 *Prehistory of the Indo-Malaysian Archipelago.* Sydney and Orlando: Academic Press.

Bernet Kempers, A. J.
1988 *The Kettledrums of Southeast Asia: A Bronze Age World and Its Aftermath.* Modern Quaternary Research in Southeast Asia, vol. 10 (1986/1987), ed. Gert-Jan Bartstra and Willem Arnold Casparie. Rotterdam and Brookfield: Balkema.

Bezemer, T. J.
n.d. *Indonesische kunstnijverheid; Indonesian Arts and Crafts.* Special publication of the periodical *Nederlandsch-Indië Oud en Nieuw.* The Hague, ca. 1931.

Boechari
1979 "An Old Malay Inscription of Srivijaya at Palas Pasemah (South Lampung)." In *Pra Seminar Penelitian Sriwijaya,* pp. 18–40. Jakarta: Pusat Penelitian Purbakala dan Peninggalan Nasional.

Brakel, J. H. van, et al.
1987 *Budaya Indonesia: Kunst en cultuur in Indonesië; Arts and Crafts in Indonesia.* Amsterdam: Tropenmuseum/ Koninklijk Instituut voor de Tropen. Exhibition catalogue.

Bühler, Alfred, and Eberhard Fischer
1979 *The Patola of Gujarat: Double Ikat in India.* 2 vols. Basel: Krebs.

Cheesman, Patricia
1988 *Lao Textiles: Ancient Symbols—Living Art.* Bangkok: White Lotus.

Delhi. Government of India
[1957] *The Way of the Buddha.* Delhi: Publications Division, Ministry of Information and Broadcasting. Published on the occasion of the 2500th anniversary of the Mahaparinirvana of the Buddha.

Downs, R. E.
1955 "Head-hunting in Indonesia." *Bijdragen tot de Taal-, Land- en Volkenkunde,* no. 111, pp. 40–70. Leiden: Koninklijk Instituut voor Taal-, Land- en Volkenkunde. Reprinted in *Structural Anthropology in the Netherlands,* ed. P. E. de Josselin de Jong, pp. 117–49. Koninklijk Instituut voor Taal-, Land- en Volkenkunde, Leiden, translation series 17. The Hague: Nijhoff, 1977.

1956 *The Religion of the Bare'e-Speaking Toradja of Central Celebes.* The Hague: Excelsior.

Feldbauer, Sergio
1988 *Bathik: Simboli magici e tradizione femminile a Giava.* Milan: Electa. Exhibition catalogue.

Forth, Gregory L.
1981 *Rindi: An Ethnographic Study of a Traditional Domain in Eastern Sumba.* Verhandelingen van het Koninklijk Instituut voor Taal-, Land- en Volkenkunde, Leiden, no. 93. The Hague: Nijhoff.

Galis, K. W., D. C. Mulder, and A. F. Ros
1970 *Java: Religie en kunst.* Delft: Ethnografisch Museum Delft. Exhibition catalogue.

Gittinger, Mattiebelle S.
1972 "A Study of the Ship Cloths of South Sumatra: Their Design and Usage." Ph.D. diss., Columbia University, New York.

1979 *Splendid Symbols: Textiles and Tradition in Indonesia.* Washington, D.C.: Textile Museum. Exhibition catalogue. 2nd expanded ed., Singapore: Oxford University Press, 1985.

1980 "Indonesian Textiles." *Arts of Asia* (Hong Kong) 10, no. 5 (September–October), pp. 108–23.

1985 Public lecture, Symposium on Indonesian Textiles September 29, Rautenstrauch-Joest-Museum für Völkerkunde, Cologne.

1989 "A Reassessment of the *Tampan* of South Sumatra." In *To Speak with Cloth: Contributions to Indonesian Textile Studies*, ed. Mattiebelle Gittinger. Los Angeles: Museum of Cultural History, University of California. Forthcoming.

Grubauer, Albert
1923 *Celebes: Ethnologische Streifzüge in Südost- und Zentral-Celebes.* Hagen and Darmstadt: Folkwang-Verlag.

Guy, John S.
1987 "Commerce, Power, and Mythology: Indian Textiles in Indonesia." *Indonesia Circle* 42 (March), pp. 57–75. London: School of Oriental and African Studies.

Haddon, Alfred C., and Laura E. Start
1936 *Iban or Sea Dayak Fabrics and Their Patterns: A Descriptive Catalogue of the Iban Fabrics in the Museum of Archaeology and Ethnology, Cambridge.* Cambridge: The University Press.

Hardjonagoro, K. R. T.
1980 "The Place of Batik in the History and Philosophy of Javanese Textiles: A Personal View," trans. and ed. R. J. Holmgren. In *Indonesian Textiles: Irene Emery Roundtable on Museum Textiles, 1979 Proceedings*, ed. Mattiebelle Gittinger, pp. 223–42. Washington, D.C.: Textile Museum.

Heekeren, H. R. van
1972 *The Stone Age of Indonesia.* 2nd rev. ed. Verhandelingen van het Koninklijk Instituut voor Taal-, Land- en Volkenkunde, Leiden, no. 61. The Hague: Nijhoff.

Holmgren, Robert J.
1979 "The Spirited Textiles of the Indonesian Archipelago." *Asia* 1, no. 6 (March–April), pp. 24–32. New York: Asia Society.

1983 Public lecture, The Irene Emery Roundtable on Museum Textiles: The Eastern Hemisphere Textile Trade. September 7–8, Indianapolis Museum of Art.

Holmgren, Robert J., and Anita E. Spertus
1980 "*Tampan pasisir*: Pictorial Documents of an Ancient Indonesian Coastal Culture." In *Indonesian Textiles: Irene Emery Roundtable on Museum Textiles, 1979 Proceedings*, ed. Mattiebelle Gittinger, pp. 157–98. Washington, D.C.: Textile Museum.

1989a "Is *Gĕringsing* Really Balinese?" In *Symposium on Indonesian Textiles.* Cologne: Rautenstrauch-Joest-Museum für Völkerkunde. Forthcoming.

1989b "Newly Discovered *Patola* Motif Types: Extensions to Bühler and Fischer, *The Patola of Gujarat.*" In *Symposium on Indonesian Textiles.* Cologne: Rautenstrauch-Joest-Museum für Völkerkunde. Forthcoming.

Holmgren, Robert J., et al.
1991 *Lampung: Art of an Old Indonesian Culture.* Forthcoming.

Honolulu Academy of Arts
1989 *Honolulu Academy of Arts: Selected Works.* Honolulu. Forthcoming.

Howell, William
1963 "The Sea Dayaks." In *The Sea Dayaks and Other Races of Sarawak*, ed. Anthony Richards, pp. 1–5. Kuching: Borneo Literature Board. Reprinted from *The Sarawak Gazette*, 1898.

Jager Gerlings, J. H.
1952 *Sprekende weefsels: Studie over ontstaan en betekenis van weefsels van enige Indonesische eilanden; Telling ᵎ Study on the Origin and Meaning of Textiles of S Indonesian Islands.* Amsterdam: Scheltens & Giltay.

[Jakarta]. Koninklijk Bataviaasch Genootschap van Kunsten en Wetenschappen
1940 *Jaarboek* 7. Bandoeng: A. C. Nix.

[Jakarta]. Koninklijk Nederlandsch Aardrijkskundig Genootschap
1938 *Atlas van Tropisch Nederland.* Batavia: Topografischen Dienst in Nederlandsch-Indië.

Kartiwa, Suwati
1987 *Tenun Ikat; Indonesian Ikats.* Jakarta: Djambatan.

Kartiwa, Suwati, Sumarah Adhyatman, Redjeki Zainul Arifin, and S. J. H. Damais
1976 *Kain Adat; Traditional Textiles.* Jakarta: Himpunan Wastraprema.

Kaudern, Walter
1944 *Art in Central Celebes.* Vol. 6 of *Ethnographical Studies in Celebes.* Ed. Teres Kaudern and Henry Wassén. Göteborg: Elanders Boktryckeri Aktiebolag.

Kazak Folk Art Designs Editorial Board
1980 *A Collection of the Kazak Folk Art Designs.* [Xinjiang]: Xinjiang People's Publishing House.

Khan Majlis, Brigitte
1984 *Indonesische Textilien: Wege zu Göttern und Ahnen.* Cologne: Rautenstrauch-Joest-Museum für Völkerkunde. Exhibition catalogue.

Kooijman, Simon
1963 *Ornamented Bark-Cloth in Indonesia.* Mededelingen van het Rijksmuseum voor Volkenkunde, no. 16. Leiden: Brill.

Kruyt, Albert C.
1938 *De West-Toradjas op Midden-Celebes*. 5 vols. Verhandelingen der Koninklijke Nederlandsche Akademie van Wetenschappen (Afdeling Letterkunde), new series 40. Amsterdam.

Langewis, Laurens, and Frits A. Wagner
1964 *Decorative Art in Indonesian Textiles*. Amsterdam: Van der Peet.

Manguin, Pierre-Yves
1986 "Shipshape Sociéties: Boat Symbolism and Political Systems in Insular Southeast Asia." In *Southeast Asia in the 9th to 14th Centuries*, ed. David G. Marr and A. C. Milner, pp. 187–213. Singapore: Institute of Southeast Asian Studies.

Maxwell, Robyn
1990 *Tradition, Trade, and Transformation: Textiles of Southeast Asia*. Canberra: Australian National Gallery. Forthcoming.

Milne, Mrs. Leslie [Mary Lewis]
1910 *Shans at Home*. London: Murray.

Nooy-Palm, Hetty
1970 "Dress and Adornment of the Sa'dan-Toradja (Celebes, Indonesia)." *Tropical Man* (Yearbook of the Department of Social Research, Royal Tropical Institute, Amsterdam) 2 (1969), pp. 162–94. Leiden: Brill.

1975 *De karbouw en de kandaure*. Delft: Indonesisch Ethnografisch Museum. Exhibition catalogue.

1979 *The Sa'dan-Toraja: A Study of Their Social Life and Religion*. Vol. 1, *Organization, Symbols, and Beliefs*. Verhandelingen van het Koninklijk Instituut voor Taal-, Land- en Volkenkunde, Leiden, no. 87. The Hague: Nijhoff.

1980 "The Role of the Sacred Cloths in the Mythology and Ritual of the Sa'dan Toraja of Sulawesi, Indonesia." In *Indonesian Textiles: Irene Emery Roundtable on Museum Textiles, 1979 Proceedings*, ed. Mattiebelle Gittinger, pp. 81–95. Washington, D.C.: Textile Museum.

1986 *The Sa'dan-Toraja: A Study of Their Social Life and Religion*. Vol. 2, *Rituals of the East and West*. Verhandelingen van het Koninklijk Instituut voor Taal-, Land- en Volkenkunde, Leiden, no. 118. Dordrecht: Foris Publications.

Nouhuys, J. W. van
1921 "Een autochthoon weefgebied in Midden-Celebes." *Nederlandsch-Indië Oud en Nieuw* (The Hague) 6 (December), pp. 237–43.

1925 "Was-batik in Midden-Celebes." *Nederlandsch-Indië Oud en Nieuw* (The Hague) 10 (August), pp. 110–22.

Pal, Pratapaditya
1975 *Nepal: Where the Gods Are Young*. New York: Asia Society. Exhibition catalogue.

Pigeaud, Theodore G. Th.
1938 *Javaanse volksvertoningen*. Batavia: Volkslectuur.

1967 *Literature of Java*. Vol. 1, *Synopsis of Javanese Literature, 900–1900 A.D.* Leiden and The Hague: Koninklijk Instituut voor Taal-, Land- en Volkenkunde and Nijhoff.

Rassers, W. H.
1959 *Pañji, the Culture Hero: A Structural Study of Religion in Java*. Koninklijk Instituut voor Taal-, Land- en Volkenkunde, Leiden, translation series 3. The Hague: Nijhoff.

Rodgers, Susan
1985 *Power and Gold: Jewelry from Indonesia, Malaysia, and the Philippines from the Collection of the Barbier-Müller Museum Geneva*. Geneva: Barbier-Müller Museum. Exhibition catalogue.

Rotterdam. Museum voor Land- en Volkenkunde
1965 *Indonesië-Oceanië: Kunst uit particulier bezit*. Rotterdam. Exhibition catalogue.

Royen, Josephus W. van
1930 *Nota over de Lampoengsche merga's*. Weltevreden: Landsdrukkerij.

Sarasin, Paul and Fritz
1905 *Reisen in Celebes ausgeführt in den Jahren 1893–1896 und 1902–1903*. 2 vols. Weisbaden: Kreidel.

Schärer, Hans
1942 "Die Vorstellungen der Ober- und Unterwelt bei den Ngadju Dajak von Süd-Borneo." *Cultureel Indië* 4, pp. 73–81. Leiden: Brill.

1963 *Ngaju Religion: The Conception of God among a South Borneo People*. Koninklijk Instituut voor Taal-, Land- en Volkenkunde, Leiden, translation series 6. The Hague: Nijhoff. Originally published as *Die Gottesidee der Ngadju Dajak in Süd-Borneo*. Leiden: Brill, 1946.

Schuster, Carl
1965 "Remarks on the Design of an Early Ikat Textile in Japan." In *Festschrift Alfred Bühler*, pp. 339–68. Basler Beiträge zur Geographie und Ethnologie, Ethnologische Reihe, 2. Basel: Pharos.

Solyom, Garrett and Bronwen
1984 *Fabric Traditions of Indonesia*. Pullman: Washington State University Press. Exhibition catalogue.

Steinmann, Alfred
1946 "The Ship of the Dead in Textile Art." *Ciba Review* (Basel), no. 52 (September), pp. 1870–96.

Suchtelen, B. C. C. M. M. van
1919 *Nota Endeh*. Weltevreden: Encyclopaedisch Bureau.

Tillmann, Georg
1938a "Iets over de weefsels van de Kroë districten in Zuid-Sumatra." *Maandblad voor Beeldende Kunsten* 15, no. 1 (January), pp. 10–16, 30–31. Amsterdam: De Bussy.

1938b "Iets over de weefsels van de Lampong'sche districten in Zuid-Sumatra." *Maandblad voor Beeldende Kunsten* 15, no. 5 (May), pp. 130–43. Amsterdam: De Bussy.

Veen, H. van der
1965 *The Merok Feast of the Sa'dan Toradja*. Verhandelingen van het Koninklijk Instituut voor Taal-, Land- en Volkenkunde, Leiden, no. 45. The Hague: Nijhoff.

1966 *The Sa'dan Toradja Chant for the Deceased*. Verhandelingen van het Koninklijk Instituut voor Taal-, Land- en Volkenkunde, Leiden, no. 49. The Hague: Nijhoff.

Veldhuisen-Djajasoebrata, Alit
1984 *Bloemen van het heelal: De kleurrijke wereld van de textiel op Java*. Amsterdam and Rotterdam: Sijthoff and Museum voor Land- en Volkenkunde.

Vogelsanger, Cornelia
1980 "A Sight for the Gods: Notes on the Social and Religious Meaning of Iban Ritual Fabrics." In *Indonesian Textiles: Irene Emery Roundtable on Museum Textiles, 1979 Proceedings*, ed. Mattiebelle Gittinger, pp. 115–26. Washington, D.C.: Textile Museum.

Watters, Kent
n.d. "*Sungkit* Weaving of the Iban." *Connaissance des Arts Tribaux* 9, unpaged. Geneva: L'Association des Amis du Musée Barbier-Müller.

Wheatley, Paul
1983 *Nagara and Commandery: Origins of the Southeast Asian Urban Tradition*. Department of Geography Research Paper, nos. 207–8. Chicago: Department of Geography, University of Chicago.

Wilkinson, R. J.
1957 *A Malay-English Dictionary (Romanised)*. Facsimile of the 1923 ed. 2 vols. London: Macmillan.

Yoshimoto Shinobu
1977–78 *Indoneshia senshoku taikei* (Survey of Indonesian dyeing and weaving). 2 vols. Kyoto: Shikosha.

Yoshioka Tsuneo and Yoshimoto Shinobu
1980 *Sarasa no sekai; Sarasa of the World: Indian Chintz, European Print, Batik, Japanese Stencil*. Kyoto: Shikosha.

Zoetmulder, P. J.
1982 *Old Javanese-English Dictionary*. In collaboration with S. O. Robson. 2 vols. The Hague: Nijhoff.